The Spirit of America

Henry Van Dyke

Alpha Editions

This edition published in 2024

ISBN : 9789361474248

Design and Setting By
Alpha Editions
www.alphaedis.com
Email - info@alphaedis.com

As per information held with us this book is in Public Domain.
This book is a reproduction of an important historical work. Alpha Editions uses the best technology to reproduce historical work in the same manner it was first published to preserve its original nature. Any marks or number seen are left intentionally to preserve its true form.

Contents

PREFACE .... - 1 -

INTRODUCTION .... - 2 -

I THE SOUL OF A PEOPLE .... - 5 -

II SELF-RELIANCE AND THE REPUBLIC .... - 18 -

III FAIR PLAY AND DEMOCRACY .... - 36 -

IV WILL-POWER, WORK, AND WEALTH .... - 55 -

V COMMON ORDER AND SOCIAL COÖPERATION ..... - 72 -

VI PERSONAL DEVELOPMENT AND EDUCATION ...... - 93 -

VII SELF-EXPRESSION AND LITERATURE .... - 114 -

PREFACE

This book contains the first seven of a series of twenty-six *conférences*, given in the winter of 1908-1909, on the Hyde Foundation, at the University of Paris, and repeated in part at other universities of France. They were delivered in English, and afterward translated into French and published under the title of *Le Génie de l'Amérique*. In making this American edition it has not seemed worth while to attempt to disguise the fact that these chapters were prepared as lectures to be given to a French audience, and that their purpose, in accordance with the generous design of the founder of the chair, was to promote an intelligent sympathy between France and the United States. If the book finds readers among my countrymen, I beg them, as they read, to remember its origin. Perhaps it may have an interest of its own, as a report, made in Paris, of the things that seem vital, significant, and creative in the life and character of the American people.

INTRODUCTION

There is an ancient amity between France and America, which is recorded in golden letters in the chronicles of human liberty. In one of the crowded squares of New York there stands a statue of a young nobleman, slender, elegant, and brave, springing forward to offer his sword to the cause of freedom. The name under that figure is La Fayette. In one of the broad avenues of Paris there stands a statue of a plain gentleman, grave, powerful, earnest, sitting his horse like a victor and lifting high his sword to salute the star of France. The name under that figure is Washington.

It is well that in both lands such a friendship between two great peoples should be

"Immortalized by art's immortal praise."

It is better still that it should be warmed and strengthened by present efforts for the common good: that the world should see the two great republics standing together for justice and fair play at Algeciras, working together for the world's peace at the Congress of the Hague.

But in order that a friendship like this should really continue and increase, there must be something more than a sentimental sympathy. There must be a mutual comprehension, a real understanding, between the two peoples. Romantic love, the little *Amor* with the bow and arrows, may be as blind as the painters and novelists represent him. But true friendship, the strong god *Amicitia*, is open-eyed and clear-sighted. So long as Frenchmen insist upon looking at America merely as the country of the Sky-scraper and the Almighty Dollar, so long as Americans insist upon regarding France merely as the home of the Yellow Novel and the Everlasting Dance, so long will it be difficult for the ancient amity between these two countries to expand and deepen into a true and vital concord.

France and America must know each other better. They must learn to look each into the other's mind, to read each the other's heart. They must recognize each other less by their foibles and more by their faiths, less by the factors of national weakness and more by the elements of national strength. Then, indeed, I hope and believe they will be good and faithful friends.

It is to promote this serious and noble purpose that an American gentleman, Mr. James Hazen Hyde, has founded two chairs, one at the University of Paris, and one at Harvard University, for an annual interchange of professors, (and possibly of ideas,) between France and

America. Through this generous arrangement we have had the benefit of hearing, in the United States, MM. Doumic, Rod, de Régnier, Gaston Deschamps, Hugues Le Roux, Mabilleau, Anatole Leroy-Beaulieu, Millet, Le Braz, Tardieu, and the Vicomte d'Avenel. On the same basis Messrs. Barrett Wendell, Santayana, Coolidge, and Baker have spoken at the Sorbonne and at the other French Universities. This year Harvard has called me from the chair of English Literature at Princeton University, and the authorities of the Sorbonne have graciously accorded me the hospitality of this *Amphithéâtre Richelieu*, to take my small part in this international mission.

Do you ask for my credentials as an ambassador? Let me omit such formalities as academic degrees, professorships, and doctorates, and present my claims in more simple and humble form. A family residence of two hundred and fifty years in America, whither my ancestors came from Holland in 1652; a working life of thirty years which has taken me among all sorts and conditions of men, in almost all the states of the Union from Maine to Florida and from New York to California; a personal acquaintance with all the Presidents except one since Lincoln; a friendship with many woodsmen, hunters, and fishermen in the forests where I spend the summers; an entire independence of any kind of political, ecclesiastical, or academic partisanship; and some familiarity with American literature, its origins, and its historical relations,—these are all the claims that I can make to your attention. They are small enough, to be sure, but such as they are you may find in them a partial explanation of the course which these lectures are to take.

You will understand that if I have chosen a subject which is not strictly academic, it is because the best part of my life has been spent out of doors among men. You will perceive that my failure to speak of Boston as the centre of the United States may have some connection with the accident that I am not a Bostonian. You will account for the absence of a suggestion that any one political party is the only hope of the Republic by the fact that I am not a politician. You will detect in my attitude towards literature the naïve conviction that it is not merely an art existing for art's sake, but an expression of the inner life and a factor in the moral character. Finally, you will conclude, with your French logicality of mind, that I must be an obstinate idealist, because I am going to venture to lecture to you on *The Spirit of America*. That is as much as to say that I believe man is led by an inner light, and that the ideals, moral convictions, and vital principles of a people are the most important factors in their history.

All these things are true. They cannot be denied or concealed. I would willingly confess them and a hundred more, if I might contribute but a little towards the purpose of these lectures: to help some of the people of France to understand more truly the real people of America,—a people of idealists engaged in a great practical task.

I
THE SOUL OF A PEOPLE

There is a proverb which affirms that in order to know a man you have only to travel with him for a week. Almost all of us have had experiences, sometimes happy and sometimes the reverse, which seem to confirm this saying.

A journey in common is a sort of involuntary confessional. There is a certain excitement, a confusion and quickening of perceptions and sensations, in the adventures, the sudden changes, the new and striking scenes of travel. The bonds of habit are loosened. Impulses of pleasure and of displeasure, suddenly felt, make themselves surprisingly visible. Wishes and appetites and prejudices which are usually dressed in a costume of words so conventional as to amount to a disguise now appear unmasked, and often in very scanty costume, as if they had been suddenly called from their beds by an alarm of fire on a steamboat, or, to use a more agreeable figure, by the announcement in a hotel on the Righi of approaching sunrise.

There is another thing which plays, perhaps, a part in this power of travel to make swift disclosures. I mean the vague sense of release from duties and restraints which comes to one who is away from home. Much of the outward form of our daily conduct is regulated by the structure and operation of the social machinery in which we quite inevitably find our place. But when all this is left behind, when a man no longer feels the pressure of the neighbouring wheels, the constraint of the driving-belt which makes them all move together, nor the restraint of the common task to which the collective force of all is applied, he is "outside of the machine."

The ordinary sight-seeing, uncommercial traveller—the tourist, the globe-trotter—is not usually a person who thinks much of his own responsibilities, however conscious he may be of his own importance. His favourite proverb is, "When you are in Rome, do as the Romans do." But in the application of the proverb, he does not always inquire whether the particular thing which he is invited to do is done by the particular kind of Roman that he would like to be, if he lived in Rome, or by some other kind of Roman quite different, even contrary. He is liberated. He is unaccountable. He is a butterfly visiting a strange garden. He has only to enjoy himself according to his caprice and to accept the invitations of the flowers which please him most.

This feeling of irresponsibility in travel corresponds somewhat to the effect of wine. The tongue is loosened. Unexpected qualities and inclinations are unconsciously confessed. A new man, hitherto unknown, appears upon the scene. And this new man often seems more natural, more spontaneous, more vivid, than our old acquaintance. "At last," we say to ourselves, "we know the true inwardness, the real reality of this fellow. He is not acting a part now. He is coming to the surface. We see what a bad fellow, or what a good fellow, he is. *In vino et in viatore veritas!*"

But is it quite correct, after all, this first impression that travel is the great revealer of character? Is it the essential truth, the fundamental truth, *la vraie verité*, that we discover through this glass? Or is it, rather, a novel aspect of facts which are real enough, indeed, but not fundamental,—an aspect so novel that it presents itself as more important than it really is? To put the question in brief, and in a practical form, is a railway train the place to study character, or is it only a place to observe characteristics?

There is, of course, a great deal of complicated and quarrelsome psychology involved in this seeming simple question,—for example, the point at issue between the determinists and libertarians, the philosophers of the unconscious and the philosophers of the ideal,—all of which I will prudently pass by, in order to make a very practical and common-sense observation.

Ordinary travel usually obscures and confuses quite as much as it reveals in the character of the traveller. His excitement, his moral detachment, his intellectual dislocation, unless he is a person of extraordinary firmness and poise, are apt to make him lose himself much more than they help him to find himself. In these strange and transient experiences his action lacks meaning and relation. He is carried away. He is uprooted. He is swept along by the current of external novelty. This may be good for him or bad for him. I do not ask this question. I am not moralizing. I am observing. The point is that under these conditions I do not see the real man more clearly, but less clearly. To paraphrase a Greek saying, I wish not to study Philip when he is a little exhilarated, but Philip when he is sober: not when he is at a Persian banquet, but when he is with his Macedonians.

Moreover, if I mistake not, the native environment, the chosen or accepted task, the definite place in the great world-work, is part of the man himself. There are no human atoms. Relation is inseparable from quality. Absolute isolation would be invisibility. Displacement is deformity. You remember what Emerson says in his poem, *Each and All*:—

"The delicate shells lay on the shore:
The bubbles of the latest wave
Fresh pearls to their enamel gave,
And the bellowing of the savage sea
Greeted their safe escape to me.
I wiped away the weeds and foam,
I fetched my sea-born treasures home,
But the poor, unsightly, noisome things
Had left their beauty on the shore
With the sun and the sand and the wild uproar."

So I would see my man where he belongs, in the midst of the things which have produced him and which he has helped to produce. I would understand something of his relation to them. I would watch him at his work, the daily labour which not only earns his living but also moulds and forms his life. I would see how he takes hold of it, with reluctance or with alacrity, and how he regards it, with honour or with contempt. I would consider the way in which he uses its tangible results; to what purpose he applies them; for what objects he spends the fruit of his toil; what kind of bread he buys with the sweat of his brow or his brain. I would trace in his environment the influence of those who have gone before him. I would read the secrets of his heart in the uncompleted projects which he forms for those who are to come after him. In short, I would see the roots from which he springs, and the hopes in which his heart flowers.

Thus, and thus only, the real man, the entire man, would become more clear to me. He might appear more or less admirable. I might like him more, or less. That would make no difference. The one thing that is sure is that I should know him better. I should know the soul of the man.

If this is true, then, of the individual, how much more is it true of a nation, a people? The inward life, the real life, the animating and formative life of a people is infinitely difficult to discern and understand.

There are a hundred concourses of travel in modern Europe where you may watch "the passing show" of all nations with vast amusement,—on the *Champs-Elysées* in May or June, in the park of *Aix-les-Bains* in midsummer, at the Italian Lakes in autumn, in the colonnade of Shepherd's Hotel at Cairo in January or February, on the Pincian Hill at Rome in March or April. Take your seats, ladies and gentlemen, at this continuous performance, this international *vaudeville*, and observe British habits, French manners, German customs, American eccentricities, whatever interests you in the varied entertainment. But do not imagine that in this way you will learn to know the national personality of England, or France, or Germany, or America. That is something which is never exported.

Some drop of tincture or extract of it, indeed, may pass from one land to another in a distinct and concentrated individuality, as when a Lafayette comes to America, or a Franklin to France. Some partial portrait and imperfect image of it, indeed, may be produced in literature. And there the reader who is wise enough to separate the head-dress from the head, and to discern the figure beneath the costume, may trace at least some features of the real life represented and expressed in poem or romance, in essay or discourse. But even this literature, in order to be vitally understood, must be interpreted in relation to the life of the men who have produced it and the men for whom it was produced.

Authors are not algebraic quantities,—X, Y, Z, &c. They express spiritual actions and reactions in the midst of a given environment. What they write is in one sense a work of art, and therefore to be judged accurately by the laws of that art. But when this judgment is made, when the book has been assigned its rank according to its substance, its structure, its style, there still remains another point of view from which it is to be considered. The book is a document of life. It is the embodiment of a spiritual protest, perhaps; or it is the unconscious confession of an intellectual ambition; or it is an appeal to some popular sentiment; or it is the expression of the craving for some particular form of beauty or joy; or it is a tribute to some personal or social excellence; or it is the record of some vision of perfection seen in

> "The light that never was, on sea or land,
> The consecration, and the poet's dream."

In every case, it is something that comes out of a heritage of ideals and adds to them.

The possessor of this heritage is the soul of a people. This soul of a people lives at home.

It is for this reason that America has been imperfectly understood, and in some respects positively misunderstood in Europe. The American tourists, who have been numerous (and noticeable) on all the European highways of pleasure and byways of curiosity during the last forty years, have made a vivid impression on the people of the countries which they have visited. They are recognized. They are remembered. It is not necessary to inquire whether this recognition contains more of admiration or of astonishment, whether the forms which it often takes are flattering or the reverse. On this point I am sufficiently American myself to be largely indifferent. But the point on which I feel strongly is that the popular impression of America which is derived only or chiefly from the observation of American travellers is, and must be, deficient, superficial, and in many ways misleading.

If this crowd of American travellers were a hundred times as numerous, it would still fail to be representative, it would still be unable to reveal the Spirit of America, just because it is composed of travellers.

I grant you that it includes many, perhaps almost all, of the different types and varieties of Americans, good, bad, and mediocre. You will find in this crowd some very simple people and some very complicated people; country folk and city folk; strenuous souls who come to seek culture and relaxed souls who come to spend money; millionnaires and school-teachers, saloon-keepers and university professors; men of the East and men of the West; Yankees, Knickerbockers, Hoosiers, Cavaliers, and Cowboys. Surely, you say, from such a large collection of samples one ought to be able to form an adequate judgment of the stuff.

But no; on the contrary, the larger the collection of samples, seen under the detaching and exaggerating conditions of travel, the more confused and the less sane and penetrating your impression will be, unless by some other means you have obtained an idea of the vital origin, the true relation, the common inheritance, and the national unity of these strange and diverse travellers who come from beyond the sea.

Understand, I do not mean to say that European scholars and critics have not studied American affairs and institutions to advantage and thrown a clear light of intelligence, of sympathy, of criticism, upon the history and life of the United States. A philosophical study like that of Tocqueville, a political study like that of Mr. James Bryce, a series of acute social observations like those of M. Paul Bourget, M. André Tardieu, M. Paul Boutmy, M. Weiller, an industrial study like that of M. d'Avenel, or a religious study like that of the Abbé Klein,—these are of great value. But they are quite apart, quite different, from the popular impression of America in Europe, an impression which is, and perhaps to some extent must naturally be, based upon the observations of Americans *en voyage*, and which by some strange hypnotism sometimes imposes itself for a while upon the American travellers themselves.

I call this the international postal-card view of America. It is often amusing, occasionally irritating, and almost always confusing. It has flashes of truth in it. It renders certain details with the accuracy of a kodak. But, like a picture made by the kodak, it has a deficient perspective and no atmosphere. The details do not fit together. They are irrelevant. They are often contradictory.

For example, you will hear statements made about America like the following:—

'The Americans worship the Almighty Dollar more than the English revere the Ponderous Pound or the French adore *les beaux écus sonnants.* *Per contra*, the Americans are foolish spendthrifts who have no sense of the real value of money.'

'America is a country without a social order. It is a house of one story, without partitions, in which all the inhabitants are on a level. *Per contra*, America is the place where class distinctions are most sharply drawn, and where the rich are most widely and irreconcilably separated from the poor.'

'The United States is a definite experiment in political theory, which was begun in 1776, and which has succeeded because of its philosophical truth and logical consistency. *Per contra*, the United States is an accident, a nation born of circumstances and held together by good fortune, without real unity or firm foundation.'

'The American race is a new creation, aboriginal, autochthonous, which ought to express itself in totally new and hitherto unheard-of forms of art and literature. *Per contra*, there is no American race, only a vast and absurd *mélange* of incongruous elements, cast off from Europe by various political convulsions, and combined by the pressure of events, not into a people, but into a mere population, which can never have a literature or an art of its own.'

'America is a lawless land, where every one does what he likes and pays no attention to the opinion of his neighbour. *Per contra*, America is a land of prejudice, of interference, of restriction, where personal liberty is constantly invaded by the tyranny of narrow ideas and traditions, embodied in ridiculous laws which tell a man how many hours a day he may work, what he may drink, how he may amuse himself on Sunday, and how fast he may drive his automobile.'

'Finally, America is the home of materialism, a land of crude, practical worldliness, unimaginative, irreverent, without religion. But *per contra*, America is the last refuge of superstition, of religious enthusiasm, of unenlightened devotion, even of antique bigotry, a land of spiritual dreamers and fanatics, who, as Brillat-Savarin said, have "forty religions and only one sauce."'

Have I sharpened these contrasts and contradictions a little? Have I overaccented the inconsistencies in this picture postal-card view of America?

Perhaps so. Yet it is impossible to deny that the main features of this incoherent view are familiar. We see the reflection of them in the singular choice and presentation of the rare items of American news which find their way into the columns of European newspapers. We recognize them in the talk of the street and of the *table-d'hôte*.

I remember very well the gravity and earnestness with which a learned German asked me, some years ago, whether, if he went to America, it would be a serious disadvantage to him in the first social circles to eat with his knife at the dinner-table. He was much relieved by my assurance that no one would take notice of it.

I recall also the charming naïveté with which an English lady inquired, "Have you any good writers in the States?" The answer was: "None to speak of. We import most of our literature from Australia, by way of the Cape of Good Hope."

Sometimes we are asked whether we do not find it a great disadvantage to have no language of our own; or whether the justices of the Supreme Court are usually persons of good education; or whether we often meet Buffalo Bill in New York society; or whether Shakespeare or Bernard Shaw is most read in the States. To such inquiries we try to return polite answers, although our despair of conveying the truth sometimes leads us to clothe it in a humorous disguise.

But these are minor matters. It is when we are seriously interrogated about the prospect of a hereditary nobility in America, created from the descendants of railway princes, oil magnates, and iron dukes; or when we are questioned as to the probability that the next President, or the one after the next, may assume an imperial state and crown, or perhaps that he may abolish the Constitution and establish communism; or when we are asked whether the Germans, or the Irish, or the Scandinavians, or the Jews are going to dominate the United States in the twentieth century; or when we are told that the industrial and commercial forces which created the republic are no longer coöperant but divisive, and that the nation must inevitably split into several fragments, more or less hostile, but certainly rival; it is when such questions are gravely asked, that we begin to feel that there are some grave misconceptions, or at least that there is something important lacking, in the current notion of how America came into being and what America really is.

I believe that the thing which is lacking is the perception of the Spirit of America as the creative force, the controlling power, the characteristic element of the United States.

The republic is not an accident, happy or otherwise. It is not a fortuitous concourse of emigrants. It is not the logical demonstration of an abstract theory of government. It is the development of a life,—an inward life of ideals, sentiments, ruling passions, embodying itself in an outward life of forms, customs, institutions, relations,—a process as vital, as spontaneous, as inevitable, as the growth of a child into a man. The soul of a people has made the American nation.

It is of this Spirit of America, in the past and in the present, and of some of its expressions, that I would speak in these conferences. I speak of it in the past because I believe that we must know something of its origins, its early manifestations, its experiences, and its conflicts in order to understand what it truly signifies.

The spirit of a people, like the spirit of a man, is influenced by heredity. But this heredity is not merely physical, it is spiritual. There is a transmission of qualities through the soul as well as through the flesh. There is an intellectual paternity. There is a kinship of the mind as well as of the body. The soul of the people in America to-day is the lineal descendant of the soul of the people which made America in the beginning.

Just at what moment of time this soul came into being, I do not know. Some theologians teach that there is a certain point at which the hidden physical life of an infant receives a *donum* of spiritual life which makes it a person, a human being. I do not imagine that we can fix any such point in the conception and gestation of a people. Certainly it would be difficult to select any date of which we could say with assurance, "On that day, in that year, the exiles of England, of Scotland, of Holland, of France, of Germany, on the shores of the new world, became one folk, into which the Spirit of America entered." But just as certainly it is clear that the mysterious event came to pass. And beyond a doubt the time of its occurrence was long before the traditional birthday of the republic, the 4th of July, 1776.

The Declaration of Independence did not create—it did not even pretend to create—a new state of things. It simply recognized a state of things already existing. It declared "that these United Colonies *are*, and of right ought to be, free and independent States."

The men who framed this declaration were not ignorant, nor careless in the use of words. When practically the same men were called, a few years later, to frame a constitution for the United States, they employed quite different language: "We, the people of the United States, ... do ordain and establish this Constitution." That is the language of creation. It assumes to bring into being something which did not previously exist. But the language of the Declaration of Independence is the language of recognition. It sets forth clearly a fact which has already come to pass, but which has hitherto been ignored, neglected or denied.

What was that fact? Nothing else than the existence of a new people, separate, distinct, independent, in the thirteen American colonies. At what moment in the troubled seventeenth century, age of European revolt and conflict, the spirit of liberty brooding upon the immense wilderness of the New World, engendered this new life, we cannot tell. At what moment in the philosophical eighteenth century, age of reason and reflection, this new life began to be self-conscious and to feel its way toward an organic unity of powers and efforts, we cannot precisely determine. But the thing that is clear and significant is that independence existed before it was declared. The soul of the American people was already living and conscious before the history of the United States began.

I call this fact significant, immensely significant, because it marks not merely a verbal distinction but an essential difference, a difference which is vital to the true comprehension of the American spirit in the past and in the present.

A nation brought to birth by an act of violence, if such a thing be possible,—or let us rather say, a nation achieving liberty by a sharp and sudden break with its own past and a complete overturning of its own traditions, will naturally carry with it the marks of such an origin. It will be inclined to extreme measures and methods. It will be particularly liable to counter-revolutions. It will often vibrate between radicalism and reactionism.

But a nation "conceived in liberty," to use Lincoln's glorious phrase, and pursuing its natural aims, not by the method of swift and forcible change, but by the method of normal and steady development, will be likely to have another temperament and a different history. It will at least endeavour to practice moderation, prudence, patience. It will try new experiments slowly. It will advance, not indeed without interruption, but with a large and tranquil confidence that its security and progress are in accordance with the course of nature and the eternal laws of right reason.

Now this is true in the main of the United States. And the reason for this large and tranquil confidence, at which Europeans sometimes smile because it looks like bravado, and for this essentially conservative temper, at which Europeans sometimes wonder because it seems unsuitable to a democracy,—the reason, I think, is to be found in the history of the soul of the people.

The American Revolution, to speak accurately and philosophically, was not a revolution at all. It was a resistance.

The Americans did not propose to conquer new rights and privileges, but to defend old ones.

The claim of Washington and Adams and Franklin and Jefferson and Jay and Schuyler and Witherspoon was that the kings of England had established the colonies in certain liberties which the Parliament was endeavouring to take away. These liberties, the Americans asserted, belonged to them not only by natural right, but also by precedent and ancient tradition. The colonists claimed that the proposed reorganization of the colonies, which was undertaken by the British Parliament in 1763, was an interruption of their history and a change in the established conditions of their life. They were unwilling to submit to it. They united and armed to prevent it. They took the position of men who were defending their inheritance of self-government against a war of subjugation disguised as a new scheme of imperial legislation.

Whether they were right or wrong in making this claim, whether the arguments by which they supported it were sound or sophistical, we need not now consider. For the present, the point is that the claim was made, and that the making of it is one of the earliest and clearest revelations of the Spirit of America.

No doubt in that struggle of defence which we are wont to call, for want of a better name, the Revolution, the colonists were carried by the irresistible force of events far beyond this position. The privilege of self-government which they claimed, the principle of "no taxation without representation," appeared to them, at last, defensible and practicable only on the condition of absolute separation from Great Britain. This separation implied sovereignty. This sovereignty demanded union. This union, by the logic of events, took the form of a republic. This republic continues to exist and to develop along the normal lines of its own nature, because it is still animated and controlled by the same Spirit of America which brought it into being to embody the soul of the people.

I am quite sure that there are few, even among Americans, who appreciate the literal truth and the full meaning of this last statement. It is common to assume that the Spirit of 1776 is an affair of the past; that the native American stock is swallowed up and lost in our mixed population;

and that the new United States, beginning, let us say, at the close of the Civil War, is now controlled and guided by forces which have come to it from without. This is not true even physically, much less is it true intellectually and morally.

The blended strains of blood which made the American people in the beginning are still the dominant factors in the American people of to-day. Men of distinction in science, art, and statesmanship have come from abroad to cast their fortunes in with the republic,—men like Gallatin and Agassiz and Guyot and Lieber and McCosh and Carl Schurz,—and their presence has been welcomed, their service received with honour. Of the total population of the United States in 1900 more than 34 per cent were of foreign birth or parentage. But the native stock has led and still leads America.

There is a popular cyclopædia of names, called *Who's Who in America*, which contains brief biographies of some 16,395 living persons, who are supposed to be more or less distinguished, in one way or another, in the various regions in which they live. It includes the representatives of foreign governments in the United States, and some foreign authors and business men. It is not necessary to imagine that all who are admitted to this quasi-golden book of "Who's-who-dom" are really great or widely famous. There are perhaps many of whom we might inquire, Which is who, and why is he somewhat? But, after all, the book includes most of the successful lawyers, doctors, merchants, bankers, preachers, politicians, authors, artists, and teachers,—the people who are most influential in their local communities and best known to their fellow-citizens. The noteworthy fact is that 86.07 per cent are native Americans. I think that a careful examination of the record would show that a very large majority have at least three generations of American ancestry on one side or the other of the family.

Of the men elected to the presidency of the United States there has been only one whose ancestors did not belong to America before the Revolution,—James Buchanan, whose father was a Scotch-Irish preacher who came to the New World in 1783. All but four of the Presidents of the United States could trace their line back to Americans of the seventeenth century.

But it is not upon these striking facts of physical heredity that I would rest my idea of an American people, distinct and continuous, beginning a conscious life at some time antecedent to 1764 and still guiding the development of the United States. I would lay far more stress upon intellectual and spiritual heredity, that strange process of moral generation by which the qualities of the Spirit of America have been communicated to millions of immigrants from all parts of the world.

Since 1820 about twenty-six million persons have come to the United States from foreign lands. At the present moment, in a population which is estimated at about ninety millions, there are probably between thirteen and fifteen millions who are foreign-born. It is an immense quantity for any nation to digest and assimilate, and it must be confessed that there are occasional signs of local dyspepsia in the large cities. But none the less it may be confidently affirmed that the foreign immigration of the past has been thoroughly transformed into American material, and that the immigration of the present is passing through the same process without any alarming interruption.

I can take you into quarters of New York where you might think yourself in a Russian Ghetto, or into regions of Pennsylvania which would seem to you like Hungarian mining towns. But if you will come with me into the public schools, where the children of these people of the Old World are gathered for education, you will find yourself in the midst of fairly intelligent and genuinely patriotic young Americans. They will salute the flag for you with enthusiasm. They will sing "Columbia" and "The Star Spangled Banner" with more vigour than harmony. They will declaim Webster's apostrophe to the Union, or cry with Patrick Henry, "Give me liberty or give me death."

What is more, they will really feel, in some dim but none the less vital way, the ideals for which these symbols stand. Give them time, and their inward allegiance will become clearer, they will begin to perceive how and why they are Americans. They will be among those wise children who know their own spiritual fathers.

Last June it fell to my lot to deliver the commencement address at the College of the City of New York, a free institution which is the crown of the public school system of the city. Only a very small proportion of the scholars had names that you could call American, or even Anglo-Saxon. They were French and German, Polish and Italian, Russian and Hebrew. Yet as I spoke on the subject of citizenship, suggested by the recent death of that great American, ex-President Grover Cleveland, the response was intelligent, immediate, unanimous, and eager. There was not one of that crowd of young men who would have denied or surrendered his right to trace his patriotic ancestry, his inherited share in the Spirit of America, back to Lincoln and Webster, Madison and Jefferson, Franklin and Washington.

Here, then, is the proposition to which I dedicate these conferences.

There is now, and there has been since before the Revolution, a Spirit of America, the soul of a people, and it is this which has made the United States and which still animates and controls them.

I shall try to distinguish and describe a few, four or five of the essential features, qualities, ideals,—call them what you will,—the main elements of that spirit as I understand it. I shall also speak of two or three other traits, matters of temperament, perhaps, more than of character, which seem to me distinctly American. Then because I am neither a politician nor a jurist, I shall pass from the important field of civil government and national institutions, to consider some of the ways in which this soul of the American people has expressed itself in education and in social effort and in literature.

In following this course I venture to hope that it may be possible to correct, or at least to modify, some of the inaccuracies and inconsistencies in the popular view of America which prevails in some quarters of Europe. Perhaps I may be able to suggest, even to Americans, some of the real sources of our national unity and strength.

"*Un Américain*" says André Tardieu, in his recent book, "*est toujours plus proche qu'on ne croit d'un contradicteur Américain.*"

Why?

That is what I hope to show in these lectures. I do not propose to argue for any creed, nor to win converts for any political theory. In these conferences I am not a propagandist, nor a preacher, nor an advocate. Not even a professor, strictly speaking. Just a man from America who is trying to make you feel the real spirit of his country, first in her life, then in her literature. I should be glad if in the end you might be able to modify the ancient proverb a little and say, *Tout comprendre, c'est un peu aimer.*

II
SELF-RELIANCE AND THE REPUBLIC

The other day I came upon a new book with a title which seemed to take a good ideal for granted: *The New American Type*.

The author began with a description of a recent exhibition of portraits in New York, including pictures of the eighteenth, nineteenth, and twentieth centuries. He was impressed with the idea that "an astonishing change had taken place in men and women between the time of President Washington and President McKinley; bodies, faces, thoughts, had all been transformed. One short stairway from the portraits of Reynolds to those of Sargent ushered in changes as if it had stretched from the first Pharaoh to the last Ptolemy." From this interesting text the author went on into an acute and sparkling discussion of the different pictures and the personalities whom they presented, and so into an attempt to define the new type of American character which he inferred from the modern portraits.

Now it had been my good fortune, only a little while before, to see another exhibition of pictures which made upon my mind a directly contrary impression. This was not a collection of paintings, but a show of living pictures: a Twelfth Night celebration, in costume, at the Century Club in New York. Four or five hundred of the best-known and most influential men in the metropolis of America had arrayed themselves in the habiliments of various lands and ages for an evening of fun and frolic. There were travellers and explorers who had brought home the robes of the Orient. There were men of exuberant fancy who had made themselves up as Roman senators or Spanish toreadors or Provençal troubadours. But most of the costumes were English or Dutch or French of the seventeenth and eighteenth centuries. The astonishing thing was that the men who wore them might easily have been taken for their own grandfathers or great-grandfathers.

There was a Puritan who might have fled from the oppressions of Archbishop Laud, a Cavalier who might have sought a refuge from the severities of Cromwell's Parliament, a Huguenot who might have escaped from the pressing attentions of Louis XIV in the Dragonnades, a Dutch burgher who might have sailed from Amsterdam in the *Goede Vrouw*. There were soldiers of the Colonial army and members of the Continental Congress who might have been painted by Copley or Stuart or Trumbull or Peale.

The types of the faces were not essentially different. There was the same strength of bony structure, the same firmness of outline, the same expression of self-reliance, varying from the tranquillity of the quiet temperament to the turbulence of the stormy temperament. They looked like men who were able to take care of themselves, who knew what they wanted, and who would be likely to get it. They had the veritable air and expression of their ancestors of one or two hundred years ago. And yet, as a matter of fact, they were intensely modern Americans, typical New Yorkers of the twentieth century.

Reflecting upon this interesting and rather pleasant experience, I was convinced that the author of *The New American Type* had allowed his imagination to run away with his judgment. No such general and fundamental change as he describes has really taken place. There have been modifications and developments and degenerations, of course, under the new conditions and influences of modern life. There have been also great changes of fashion and dress,—the wearing of mustaches and beards,—the discarding of wigs and ruffles,—the sacrifice of a somewhat fantastic elegance to a rather monotonous comfort in the ordinary costume of men. These things have confused and misled my ingenious author.

He has been bewildered also by the alteration in the methods of portraiture. He has mistaken a change in the art of the painters for a change in the character of their subjects. It is a well-known fact that something comes into a portrait from the place and the manner in which it is made. I have a collection of pictures of Charles Dickens, and it is interesting to observe how the Scotch ones make him look a little like a Scotchman, and the London ones make him look intensely English, and the American ones give him a touch of Broadway in 1845, and the photographs made in Paris have an unmistakable suggestion of the *Boulevards*. There is a great difference between the spirit and method of Reynolds, Hoppner, Latour, Vanloo, and those of Sargent, Holl, Duran, Bonnat, Alexander, and Zorn. It is this difference that helps to conceal the essential likeness of their sitters.

I was intimately acquainted with Benjamin Franklin's great-grandson, a surgeon in the American navy. Put a fur cap and knee breeches on him, and he might easily have sat for his great-grandfather's portrait. In character there was a still closer resemblance. You can see the same faces at any banquet in New York to-day that Rembrandt has depicted in his "Night-Watch," or Franz Hals in his "Banquet of the Civic Guard."

But there is something which interests me even more than this persistence of visible ancestral features in the Americans of to-day. It is the continuance from generation to generation of the main lines, the essential elements, of that American character which came into being on the Western continent.

It is commonly assumed that this character is composite, that the people who inhabit America are a mosaic, made up of fragments brought from various lands and put together rather at haphazard and in a curious pattern. This assumption misses the inward verity by dwelling too much upon the outward fact.

Undoubtedly there were large and striking differences between the grave and strict Puritans who peopled the shores of Massachusetts Bay, the pleasure-loving Cavaliers who made their tobacco plantations in Virginia, the liberal and comfortable Hollanders who took possession of the lands along the Hudson, the skilful and industrious Frenchmen who came from old Rochelle to New Rochelle, the peaceful and prudent Quakers who followed William Penn, the stolid Germans of the Rhine who made their farms along the Susquehanna, the vigorous and aggressive Scotch-Irish Presbyterians who became the pioneers of western Pennsylvania and North Carolina, the tolerant Catholics who fled from English persecution to Lord Baltimore's Maryland. But these outward differences of speech, of dress, of habits, of tradition, were, after all, of less practical consequence than the inward resemblances and sympathies of spirit which brought these men of different stocks together as one people.

They were not a composite people, but a blended people. They became in large measure conscious of the same aims, loyal to the same ideals, and capable of fighting and working together as Americans to achieve their destiny.

I suppose that the natural process of intermarriage played an important part in this blending of races. This is an affair to which the conditions of life in a new country, on the frontiers of civilization, are peculiarly favourable. Love flourishes when there are no locksmiths. In a community of exiles the inclinations of the young men towards the young women easily overstep the barriers of language and descent. Quite naturally the English and Scotch were united with the Dutch and French in the holy state of matrimony, and the mothers had as much to do as the fathers with the character-building of the children.

But apart from this natural process of combination there were other influences at work bringing the colonists into unity. There was the pressure of a common necessity—the necessity of taking care of themselves, of making their own living in a hard, new world. There was the pressure of a common danger—the danger from the fierce and treacherous savages who surrounded them and continually threatened them with pillage and slaughter. There was the pressure of a common discipline—the discipline of building up an organized industry, a civilized community in the wilderness.

Yet I doubt whether even these potent forces of compression, of fusion, of metamorphosis, would have made one people of the colonists quite so quickly, quite so thoroughly, if it had not been for certain affinities of spirit, certain ideals and purposes which influenced them all, and which made the blending easier and more complete.

Most of the colonists of the seventeenth century, you will observe, were people who in one way or another had suffered for their religious convictions, whether they were Puritans or Catholics, Episcopalians or Presbyterians, Quakers or Anabaptists.

The almost invariable effect of suffering for religion is to deepen its power and to intensify the desire for liberty to practise it.

It is true that other motives, the love of adventure, the desire to attain prosperity in the affairs of this world, and in some cases the wish to escape from the consequences of misconduct or misfortune in the old country, played a part in the settlement of America. Nothing could be more absurd than the complacent assumption that all the ancestors from whom the "Colonial Dames" or the "Sons of the Revolution" delight to trace their descent were persons of distinguished character and fervent piety.

But the most characteristic element of the early emigration was religious, and that not by convention and conformity, but by conscience and conviction. There was less difference among the various colonies in this respect than is generally imagined. The New Englanders, who have written most of the American histories, have been in the way of claiming the lion's share of the religious influence for the Puritans. But while Massachusetts was a religious colony with commercial tendencies, New Amsterdam was a commercial colony with religious principles.

The Virginia parson prayed by the book, and the Pennsylvania Quaker made silence the most important part of his ritual, but alike on the banks of the James and on the shores of the Delaware the ultimate significance and value of life were interpreted in terms of religion.

Now one immediate effect of such a ground-tone of existence is to increase susceptibility and devotion to ideals. The habit of referring constantly to religious sanctions is one that carries with it a tendency to intensify the whole motive power of life in relation to its inward conceptions of what is right and desirable. Men growing up in such an atmosphere may easily become fanatical, but they are not likely to be feeble.

Moreover, the American colonists, by the very conditions of natural selection which brought them together, must have included more than the usual proportion of strong wills, resolute and independent characters, people who knew what they wanted to do and were willing to accept needful risks and hardships in order to do it. The same thing, at least to some extent, holds good of the later immigration into the United States.

Most of the immigrants must have been rich in personal energy, clear in their conviction of what was best for them to do. Otherwise they would have lacked the force to break old ties, to brave the sea, to face the loneliness and uncertainty of life in a strange land. Discontent with their former condition acted upon them not as a depressant but as a tonic. The hope of something unseen, untried, was a stimulus to which their wills reacted. Whatever misgivings or reluctances they may have had, upon the whole they were more attracted than repelled by the prospect of shaping a new life for themselves, according to their own desire, in a land of liberty, opportunity, and difficulty.

We come thus to the first and most potent factor in the soul of the American people, *the spirit of self-reliance.* This was the dominant and formative factor of their early history. It was the inward power which animated and sustained them in their first struggles and efforts. It was deepened by religious conviction and intensified by practical experience. It took shape in political institutions, declarations, constitutions. It rejected foreign guidance and control, and fought against all external domination. It assumed the right of self-determination, and took for granted the power of self-development. In the ignorant and noisy it was aggressive, independent, cocksure, and boastful. In the thoughtful and prudent it was grave, firm, resolute, and inflexible. It has persisted through all the changes and growth of two centuries, and it remains to-day the most vital and irreducible quality in the soul of America,—*the spirit of self-reliance.*

You may hear it in its popular and somewhat vulgar form—not without a characteristic touch of humour—in the Yankee's answer to the intimation of an Englishman that if the United States did not behave themselves well, Great Britain would come over and whip them. "What!" said the Yankee, "ag'in?" You may hear it in deeper, saner, wiser tones, in Lincoln's noble asseveration on the battle-field of Gettysburg, that "government of the people, by the people, for the people *shall not* perish from the earth." But however or whenever you hear it, the thing which it utters is the same,—the inward conviction of a people that they have the right and the ability, and consequently the duty, to regulate their own life, to direct their own property, and to pursue their own happiness according to the light which they possess.

It is obvious that one may give different names to this spirit, according to the circumstances in which it is manifested and observed. It may be called the spirit of independence when it is shown in opposition to forces of external control. Professor Barrett Wendell, speaking from this chair four years ago, said that the first ideal to take form in the American consciousness was "the ideal of Liberty." But his well-balanced mind compelled him immediately to limit and define this ideal as a desire for "the political freedom of America from all control, from all coercion, from all interference by any power foreign to our own American selves." And what is this but self-reliance?

Professor Münsterberg, in his admirable book, *The Americans*, calls it "the spirit of self-direction." He traces its influence in the development of American institutions and the structure of American life. He says: "Whoever wishes to understand the secret of that baffling turmoil, the inner mechanism and motive behind all the politically effective forces, must set out from only one point. He must appreciate the yearning of the American heart after self-direction. Everything else is to be understood from this."

But this yearning after self-*direction*, it seems to me, is not peculiar to Americans. All men have more or less of it by nature. All men yearn to be their own masters, to shape their own life, to direct their own course. The difference among men lies in the clearness and the vigour with which they conceive their own right and power and duty so to do.

Back of the temper of independence, back of the passion for liberty, back of the yearning after self-direction, stands the spirit of self-reliance, from which alone they derive force and permanence. It was this spirit that made America, and it is this spirit that preserves the republic. Emerson has expressed it in a sentence: "We will walk on our own feet; we will work with our own hands; we will speak our own minds."

It is undoubtedly true that the largest influence in the development of this spirit came from the Puritans and Pilgrims of the New England colonies, bred under the bracing and strengthening power of that creed which bears the name of a great Frenchman, John Calvin, and trained in that tremendous sense of personal responsibility which so often carries with it an intense feeling of personal value and force. Yet, after all, if we look at the matter closely, we shall see that there was no very great difference among the colonists of various stocks and regions in regard to their confidence in themselves and their feeling that they both could and should direct their own affairs.

The Virginians, languishing and fretting under the first arbitrary rule of the London corporation which controlled them with military severity, obtained a "Great Charter of Privileges, Orders, and Laws" in 1618. This gave to the little body of settlers, about a thousand in number, the right of electing their own legislative assembly, and thus laid the foundation of representative government in the New World. A little later, in 1623, fearing that the former despotism might be renewed, the Virginia Assembly sent a message to the king, saying, "Rather than be reduced to live under the like government, we desire his Majesty that commissioners be sent over to hang us."

In 1624 the Virginia Company was dissolved, and the colony passed under a royal charter, but they still preserved and cherished the rights of self-rule in all local affairs, and developed an extraordinary temper of jealousy and resistance towards the real or imagined encroachments of the governors who were sent out by the king. In 1676 the Virginians practically rebelled against the authority of Great Britain because they conceived that they were being reduced to a condition of dependence and servitude. They felt confident that they were able to make their own laws and to choose their own leaders. They were distinctly not conscious of any inferiority to their brethren in England, and with their somewhat aristocratic tendencies they developed a set of men like Lee and Henry and Washington and Bland and Jefferson and Harrison, who had more real power than any of the royal governors.

In New Amsterdam, where the most liberal policy in regard to the reception of immigrants prevailed, but where for a long time there was little or no semblance of popular government, the inhabitants rebelled in 1649 against the tyranny of the agents of the Dutch West India Company which ruled them from across the sea,—ruled them fairly well, upon the whole, but still denied free play to their spirit of self-reliance. The conflicts between the bibulous and dubious Director van Twiller and his neighbours, between the fiery and arbitrary William Kieft and his Eight Men, between the valiant, obstinate, hot-tempered, and dictatorial Peter Stuyvesant and his Nine Men, have been humorously narrated by Washington Irving in his *Knickerbocker*. But underneath the burlesque chronicle of bickerings and wranglings, complaints and protests, it is easy to see the stirrings of the sturdy spirit which confides in self and desires to have control of its own affairs.

In 1649 the Vertoogh or Remonstrance of the Seven Men representing the burghers of Manhattan, Brewckelen, Amersfoort, and Pavonia was sent to the States General of the Netherlands. It demanded first that their High Mightinesses should turn out the West India Company and take direct control of New Netherland; second, that a proper municipal government should be granted to New Amsterdam; and third, that the boundaries of the province should be settled by treaty with friendly powers. This document also called attention, by way of example, to the freedom of their neighbours in New England, "where neither patrouns, nor lords, nor princes are known, but only the people." The West India Company was powerful enough to resist these demands for a time, but in 1653 New Amsterdam was incorporated as a city.

Ten years later it passed under English sovereignty, and the history of New York began. One of its first events was the protest of certain towns on Long Island against a tax which was laid upon them in order to pay for the repair of the fort in New York. They appealed to the principle of "no taxation without representation," which they claimed had been declared alike by England and by the Dutch republic. For nearly twenty years, however, this appeal and others like it were disregarded, until at last the spirit of self-reliance became irresistible. A petition was sent to the Duke of York declaring that the lack of a representative assembly was "an intolerable grievance." The Duke, it is said, was out of patience with his uneasy province, which brought him in no revenue except complaints and protests. "I have a mind to sell it," said he, "to any one who will give me a fair price." "What," cried his friend William Penn, "sell New York! Don't think of such a thing. Just give it self-government, and there will be no more trouble." The Duke listened to the Quaker, and in 1683 the first Assembly of New York was elected.

The charters which were granted by the Stuart kings to the American colonies were for the most part of an amazingly liberal character. No doubt the royal willingness to see restless and intractable subjects leave England had something to do with this liberality. But the immediate effect of it was to encourage the spirit of self-reliance. In some of the colonies, as in Connecticut and Rhode Island, the people elected their own governors as well as made their own laws. When Governor Fletcher of New York found the people of Connecticut unwilling to comply with his demands in 1693, he wrote back to England angrily: "The laws of England have no effect in this colony. They set up for a free state."

Even in those colonies where the governors and the judges were appointed by the crown, the people were quick to suspect and bitter to resent any invasion of their liberties or contradiction of their will as expressed through the popular assemblies; and these assemblies prudently retained, as a check upon executive authority, the right of voting, and paying, or not paying, the salaries of the governor and other officers.

The policy of Great Britain in regard to the American dependencies, while it vacillated somewhat, was, in the main, to leave them quite independent. Various motives may have played a part at different times in this policy. Indifference and a feeling of contempt may have had something to do with it. English liberalism and republican sympathy may have had something to do with it. A shrewd willingness to let them prosper by their own efforts, in their own way, in order that they might make a better market for English manufactures, may have had something to do with it. Thus Lord Morley tells us: "Walpole was content with seeing that no trouble came from America. He left it to the Duke of Newcastle, and the Duke left it so much to itself that he had a closet full of despatches from American governors, which had lain unopened for years."

But whatever may have been the causes of this policy, its effect was to intensify and spread the spirit of self-reliance among the people of America. A group of communities grew up along the western shore of the Atlantic which formed the habit of defending themselves, of developing their own resources, of regulating their own affairs. It has been well said that they were colonies only in the Greek sense: communities which went forth from the mother-country like children from a home, to establish a self-sustaining and equal life. They were not colonies in the Roman sense, suburbs of the empire, garrisoned and ruled from the sole centre of authority.

They felt, all of them, that they understood their own needs, their own opportunities, their own duties, their own dangers and hopes, better than any one else could understand them. "Those who feel," said Franklin, when he appeared before the committee of Parliament in London, "can best judge." They issued money, they made laws and constitutions, they raised troops, they built roads, they established schools and colleges, they levied taxes, they developed commerce,—and this last they did to a considerable extent in violation or evasion of the English laws of navigation.

They acknowledged, indeed they fervently protested, for a long time, their allegiance to Great Britain and their loyalty to the crown; but they conceived their allegiance as one of equality, and their loyalty as a voluntary sentiment largely influenced by gratitude for the protection which the king gave them in the rights of internal self-government.

This self-reliant spirit extended from the colonies into the townships and counties of which they were composed. Each little settlement, each flourishing village and small city, had its own local interests, and felt the wish and the ability to manage them. And in these communities every man was apt to be conscious of his own importance, his own value, his own ability and right to contribute to the discussion and settlement of local problems.

The conditions of life, also, had developed certain qualities in the colonists which persisted and led to a general temper of personal independence and self-confidence. The men who had cleared the forests, fought off the Indians, made homes in the wilderness, were inclined to think themselves *capable de tout*. They valued their freedom to prove this as their most precious asset.

"I have some little property in America," said Franklin. "I will freely spend nineteen shillings in the pound to defend the right of giving or refusing the other shilling; and, after all, if I cannot defend that right, I can retire cheerfully with my little family into the boundless woods of America, which are sure to furnish freedom and subsistence to any man who can bait a hook or pull a trigger." It is rather startling to think of Franklin as gaining his living as a hunter or a fisherman; but no doubt he could have done it.

The wonderful prosperity and the amazing growth of the colonies fostered this spirit of self-reliance. Their wealth was increasing more rapidly, in proportion, than the wealth of England. Their population grew from an original stock of perhaps a hundred thousand immigrants to two million in 1776, a twenty-fold advance; while in the same period of time England had only grown from five millions to eight millions, less than twofold.

The conflicts with the French power in Canada also had a powerful influence in consolidating the colonies and teaching them their strength. The first Congress in which they were all invited to take part was called in New York in 1690 to coöperate in war measures against Canada. Three long, costly, and bloody French-Indian wars, in which the colonists felt they bore the brunt of the burden and the fighting, drew them closer together, made them conscious of their common interests and of their resources.

But their victory in the last of these wars had also another effect. It opened the way for a change of policy on the part of Great Britain towards her American colonies,—a change which involved their reorganization, their subordination to the authority of the British Parliament, and the "weaving" of them, as ex-Governor Pownall put it, into "a grand marine dominion consisting of our possessions in the Atlantic and in America united into one empire, into one centre where the seat of government is." This was undoubtedly imperialism. And it was because the Americans felt this that the spirit of self-reliance rose against the new policy and stubbornly resisted every step, even the smallest, which seemed to them to lead in the direction of subjugation and dependency.

Followed ten years of acrimonious and violent controversy and eight years of war,—about what? The Stamp Act? the Paint, Paper, and Glass Act? the Tax on Tea? the Boston Port Bill?

No; but at bottom about the right and intention of the colonies to continue to direct themselves. You cannot possibly understand the

American Revolution unless you understand this. And without an understanding of the causes and the nature of the Revolution, you cannot comprehend the United States of to-day.

Take, for example, the division of opinion among the colonists themselves,—a division far more serious and far more nearly equal in numbers than is commonly supposed. It was not true, as the popular histories of the Revolution used to assume, that all the brave, the wise, the virtuous, and the honest were on one side, and all the cowardly, the selfish, the base, and the insincere were on the other. There was probably as much sincerity and virtue among the loyalists as among the patriots. There was certainly as much intelligence and education among the patriots as among the loyalists. The difference was this. The loyalists were, for the most part, families and individuals who had been connected, socially and industrially, with the royal source of power and order, through the governors and other officials who came from England or were appointed there. Naturally they felt that the protection, guidance, and support of England were indispensable to the colonies. The patriots were, for the most part, families and individuals whose intimate relations had been with the colonial assemblies, with the popular efforts for self-development and self-rule, with the movements which tended to strengthen their confidence in their own powers. Naturally they felt that freedom of action, deliverance from external control, and the fullest opportunity of self-guidance were indispensable to the colonies.

The names chosen by the two parties—"loyalist" and "patriot"—were both honourable, and seem at first sight almost synonymous. But there is a delicate shade of difference in their inward significance. The loyalist is one who sincerely owns allegiance to a sovereign power, which *may* be external to him, but to which he feels bound to be loyal. The patriot is one who has found his own country, *of which he is a part*, and for which he is willing to live and die. It was because the patriotic party appealed primarily to the spirit of self-reliance that they carried the majority of the American people with them, and won the victory, not only in the internal conflict, but also in the war of independence.

I am not ignorant nor unmindful of the part which European philosophers and political theorists played in supplying the patriotic party in America with logical arguments and philosophic reasons for the practical course which they followed. The doctrines of John Locke and Algernon Sidney were congenial and sustaining to men who had already resolved to govern themselves. From Holland aid and comfort came in the works of Grotius. Italy gave inspiration and support in the books of Beccaria and Burlamaqui on the essential principles of liberty. The French intellect, already preparing for another revolution, did much to clarify and rationalize

American thought through the sober and searching writings of Montesquieu, and perhaps even more to supply it with enthusiastic eloquence through the dithyrambic theories of Rousseau. The doctrines of natural law, and the rights of man, and the pursuit of happiness, were freely used by the patriotic orators to enforce their appeals to the people. It is impossible not to recognize the voice of the famous Genevese in the words of Alexander Hamilton: "The sacred rights of men are not to be rummaged for among old parchments or musty records. They are written as with a sunbeam in the whole volume of human nature by the hand of divinity itself, and can never be erased by mortal power."

But it still remains true that the mainspring of American independence is not to be found in any philosophic system or in any political theory. It was a vital impulse, a common sentiment in the soul of a people conscious of the ability and the determination to manage their own affairs. The logic which they followed was the logic of events and results. They were pragmatists. The spirit of self-reliance led them on, reluctantly, inevitably, step by step, through remonstrance, recalcitrance, resistance, until they came to the republic.

"Permit us to be as free as yourselves," they said to the people of Great Britain, "and we shall ever esteem a union with you to be our greatest glory and our greatest happiness." "No," answered Parliament. "Protect us as a loving father," they said to the king, "and forbid a licentious ministry any longer to riot in the ruins of mankind." "No," answered the king. "Very well, then," said the colonists, "we are, and of right ought to be, free and independent. We have governed ourselves. We are able to govern ourselves. We shall continue to govern ourselves, under such forms as we already possess; and when these are not sufficient, *we will make such forms as shall, in the opinion of the representatives of the people, best conduce to the happiness and safety of their constituents in particular and of America in general.*"

This resolution of the Continental Congress, on May 10, 1776, gives the key-note of all subsequent American history. Republicanism was not adopted because it was the only conceivable, or rational, or legitimate, form of government. It was continued, enlarged, organized, consolidated, because it was the form in which the spirit of self-reliance in the whole people found itself most at home, most happy and secure.

The federal Union of the States was established, after long and fierce argument, under the pressure of necessity, because it was evidently the only way to safeguard the permanence and freedom of those States, as well as to "establish justice, ensure domestic tranquillity, provide for the common defence, promote the general welfare, and secure the blessings of liberty to ourselves and our posterity."

The Amendments to the Constitution which were adopted in 1791 (and without the promise of which the original document never would have been accepted) were of the nature of a Bill of Rights, securing to every citizen liberty of conscience and speech, protection against arbitrary arrest, imprisonment, or deprivation of property, and especially reserving to the respective States or to the people all powers not delegated to the United States.

The division of the general government into three branches—legislative, executive, and judicial; the strict delimitation of the powers committed to these three branches; the careful provision of checks and counterchecks intended to prevent the predominance of any one branch over the others; all these are features against which political theorists and philosophers may bring, and have brought, strong arguments. They hinder quick action; they open the way to contests of authority; they are often a serious drawback in international diplomacy. But they express the purpose of a self-reliant people not to let the ultimate power pass from their hands to any one of the instruments which they have created. And for this purpose they have worked well, and are still in working order. For this reason the Americans are proud of them to a degree which other nations sometimes think unreasonable, and attached to them with a devotion which other nations do not always understand.

Do not mistake me. In saying that American republicanism is not the product of philosophical argument, of abstract theory, of reasoned conviction, I do not mean to say that Americans do not believe in it. They do.

Now and then you will find one of them who says that he would prefer a monarchy or an aristocracy. But you may be sure that he is an eccentric, or a man with a grievance against the custom-house, or a fond person who feels confident of his own place in the royal family or at least in the nobility. You may safely leave him out in trying to understand the real Spirit of America.

The people as a whole believe in the republic very firmly, and at times very passionately. And the vital reason for this belief is because it springs out of life and is rooted in life. It comes from that spirit of self-reliance which has been and is still the strongest American characteristic, in the individual, the community, and the nation.

It seems to me that we must apprehend this in order to comprehend many things that are fundamental in the life of America and the character of her people. Let me speak of a few of these things, and try to show how they have their roots in this quality of self-reliance.

Take, for example, the singular political construction of the nation,—a thing which Europeans find it almost impossible to understand without a long residence in America. It is a united country composed of States which have a distinct individual life and a carefully guarded sovereignty.

Massachusetts, New York, Virginia, Illinois, Texas, California, even the little States like Rhode Island and Maryland, are political entities just as real, just as conscious of their own being, as the United States, of which each of them forms an integral part. They have their own laws, their own courts, their own systems of domestic taxation, their own flags, their own militia, their own schools and universities. "The American citizen," Professor Münsterberg rightly says, "in daily life is first of all a member of his special State."

This distinction of local life is not to be traced to an original allegiance to different owners or lords, a duke of Savoy or Burgundy, a king of Prussia or Saxony. It is quite unlike the difference among the provinces of the French republic or the states of the German Empire. It is primarily the result of a local spirit of self-reliance, a habit of self-direction, in the people who have worked together to build up these States, to develop their resources, to give them shape and substance. This is the true explanation of State pride, and of the sense of an individual life in the different commonwealths which compose the nation.

Every one knows that this feeling was so strong immediately after the Revolution that it nearly made the Union impossible. Every one knows that this feeling was so strong in the middle of the nineteenth century that it nearly destroyed the Union. But every one does not know that this feeling is still extant and active,—an essential and potent factor in the political life of America.

The Civil War settled once for all the open and long-disputed question of the nature of the tie which binds the States together. The Union may be a compact, but it is an indissoluble compact. The United States is not a confederacy. It is a nation. Yet the local sovereignty of the States which it embraces has not been touched. The spirit of self-reliance in each commonwealth guards its rights jealously, and the law of the nation protects them.

It was but a little while ago that a proposal was made in Congress to unite the territories of Arizona and New Mexico and admit them to the Union as one State. But the people of Arizona protested. They did not wish to be mixed up with people of New Mexico, for whom they professed dislike and even contempt. They would rather stay out than come in under such conditions. The protest was sufficient to block the proposed action.

I have been reading lately a series of recent decisions by the Supreme Court, touching on various questions, like the right of one State to make the C.O.D. shipment of whiskey from another State a penal offence, or the right of the United States to interfere with the State of Colorado in the use of the water of the Arkansas River for purposes of irrigation. In all of these decisions, whether on whiskey or on water, I find that the great principle laid down by Chief Justice Marshall is clearly admitted and sustained: "The Government of the United States is one of enumerated powers." Further powers can be obtained only by a new grant from the people. "One cardinal rule," says Justice Brewer, "underlying all the relations of the States to each other is that of equality of right. Each State stands on the same level with all the rest. It can impose its own legislation on none of the others, and is bound to yield its own views to none."

Now it is evident that this peculiar structure of the nation necessarily permits, perhaps implies, a constant rivalry between two forms of the spirit of self-reliance,—the local form and the general form.

Emphasize the one, and you have a body of public opinion which moves in the direction of strengthening, enhancing, perhaps enlarging, the powers given to the central government. Emphasize the other, and you have a body of public opinion which opposes every encroachment upon the powers reserved to the local governments, and seeks to strengthen the whole by fortifying the parts of which it is composed.

Here you have the two great political parties of America. They are called to-day the Republican and the Democratic. But the names mean nothing. In fact, the party which now calls itself Democratic bore the name of Republican down to 1832; and those who were called successively Federalists and Whigs did not finally take the name of Republicans until 1860. In reality, political opinion, or perhaps it would be more correct to say political feeling, divides on this great question of the centralization or the division of power. The controversy lies between the two forms of the spirit of self-reliance; that which is embodied in the consciousness of the whole nation and that which is embodied in the consciousness of each community. The Democrats naturally speak for the latter; the Republicans for the former.

Of course in our campaigns and elections the main issue is often confused and beclouded. New problems and disputes arise in which the bearing of proposed measures is not clear. The parties have come to be great physical organizations, with vested interests to defend, with an outward life to perpetuate. Like all human institutions, both of them have the instinct of self-preservation. They both try to follow the tide of popular sentiments. They both insert planks in their platforms which seem likely to win votes. Sometimes they both hit upon the same planks, and it is very difficult to determine the original ownership.

At present, for example, the great industrial and commercial trusts and corporations are very unpopular. The Democrats and the Republicans both declare their intention to correct and restrain them. Each party claims to be the original friend of the people, the real St. George who will certainly slay the Dragon of Trusts. Thus we have had the amusing spectacle of Mr. Bryan commending and praising Mr. Roosevelt for his conversion to truly Democratic principles and policies, and adding that the Democrats were the right men to carry them out, while Mr. Taft insisted that the popular measures were essentially Republican, and that his party was the only one which could be trusted to execute them wisely and safely.

But, in spite of these temporary bewilderments, you will find, in the main, that the Republicans have a tendency towards centralizing measures, and therefore incline to favour national banks, a protective tariff, enlargement of executive functions, colonial expansion, a greater naval and military establishment, and a consequent increase of national expenditure; while the Democrats, as a rule, are on the side of non-centralizing measures, and therefore inclined to favour a large and elastic currency, free trade or tariff for revenue only, strict interpretation of the Constitution, an army and navy sufficient for police purposes, a progressive income tax, and a general policy of national economy.

The important thing to remember is that these two forms of the spirit of self-reliance, the general and the local, still exist side by side in American political life, and that it is probably a good thing to have them represented in two great parties, in order that a due balance may be kept between them.

The tendency to centralization has been in the lead, undoubtedly, during the last forty years. It is in accord with what is called the spirit of the age. But the other tendency is still deep and strong in America,—stronger I believe than anywhere else in the world. The most valuable rights of the citizen (except in territories and colonies), his personal freedom, family relations, and property, are still protected mainly by the State in which he lives and of which he is a member,—a State which is politically unknown to any foreign nation, and which exists only for the other States which are united with it!

A curious condition of affairs! Yet it is real. It is historically accountable. It belongs to the Spirit of America. For the people of that country think with Tocqueville that "Those who dread the license of the mob, and those who fear absolute power, ought alike to desire the gradual development of provincial liberties."

This is the way in which America was made. This is how Americans wish to keep it. An attempt of either party in power to destroy the principle for which the other stands would certainly fail. The day when it seemed possible to dissolve the Union is past. The day when the Union will absorb and obliterate the States is not in sight.

But it is not only in this relation of the States and the nation that you may see the workings of the spirit of which I am speaking. Within each State the spirit of self-reliance is developed and cherished in city, county, and township. Public improvements, roads and streets, police, education,— these are the important things which, as a rule, the State leaves to the local community. The city, the county, the township, attend to them. They must be paid for out of the local pocket. And the local talent of the citizens feels able and entitled to regulate them. Sometimes it is well done. Sometimes it is very badly done. But the doing of it is a privilege which a self-reliant people would be loath to resign.

Each man wishes to have his share in the discussion. The habit of argument is universal. The confidence in the ultimate judgment of the community is general. The assurance of ability to lead is frequent. And through the local office, the small task, the way lies open to larger duties and positions in the State and the nation.

It is not true that every native-born newsboy in America thinks that he *can* become President. But he knows that he *may* if he can; and perhaps it is this knowledge, or perhaps it is something in his blood, that often encourages him to try how far he can go on the way. I suppose it is true that there are more ambitious boys in America than in any other country of the world.

At the same time this spirit of self-reliance works in another and different direction. Within the seemingly complicated politics of nation, State, and town, each typical American is a person who likes to take care of himself, to have his own way, to manage his own affairs. He is not inclined to rely upon the State for aid and comfort. He wants not as much government as possible, but as little. He dislikes interference. Sometimes he resents control. He is an individual, a person, and he feels very strongly that personal freedom is what he most needs, and that he is able to make good use of a large amount of it.

Now it is evident that such a spirit as this has its weakness as well as its strength. It leads easily to overconfidence, to ignorant self-assurance, to rashness in undertaking tasks, and to careless haste in performing them.

It is good to be a person, but not good that every person should think himself a personage. It is good to be ready for any duty, but not good to undertake any duty without making ready for it.

There are many Americans who have too little respect for special training, and too much confidence in their power to solve the problems of philosophy and statesmanship extemporaneously.

No doubt there is a popular tendency to disregard exceptional powers and attainments, and to think that one man is as good as another. No doubt you can find in America some cases of self-reliance so hypertrophied that it amounts to impudence towards the laws of the universe. This is socially disagreeable, politically dangerous, and morally regrettable.

Yet we must not forget the other side. The spirit of self-reliance is not to be judged by its failures, but by its successes.

It has enabled America to assert an independence which the rest of the world, except France, thought impossible; to frame a government which the rest of the world, including France, thought impracticable; and to survive civil storms and perils which all the world thought fatal. It has animated the American people with a large and cheerful optimism which takes for granted that great things are worth doing, and tries to do them. It has made it easier to redeem a continent from the ancient wilderness and to build on new ground a civilized state sufficient to itself.

The spirit of self-reliance has fallen into mistakes, but it has shunned delays, evasions, and despairs. It has begotten explorers, pioneers, inventors. It has trained masters of industry in the school of action. It has saved the poor man from the fetters of his poverty, and delivered the lowly man from the prison of his obscurity.

Perhaps it has spoiled the worst material; but it has made the most of the average material; and it has bettered the best material. It has developed in such leaders as Franklin, Washington, Jefferson, Lincoln, Lee, Grant, and Cleveland a very noble and excellent manhood, calm, steady, equal to all emergencies.

Somehow it has brought out of the turmoil of events and conflicts the soul of an adult people, ready to trust itself and to advance into the new day without misgiving.

III
FAIR PLAY AND DEMOCRACY

It is no mistake to think of America as a democratic country. But if you wish to understand the nature and quality of the democracy which prevails there,—its specific marks, its peculiarities, and perhaps its inconsistencies,—you must trace it to its source in *the spirit of fair play*. Therefore it will be profitable to study this spirit a little more carefully, to define it a little more clearly, and to consider some illustrations of its working in American institutions, society, and character.

The spirit of fair play, in its deepest origin, is a kind of religion. It is true that religious organizations have not always shown it so that it could be identified by people outside. But this has been the fault of the organizations. At bottom, fair play is a man's recognition of the fact that he is not alone in the universe, that the world was not made for his private benefit, that the law of being is a benevolent justice which must regard and rule him as well as his fellow-men with sincere impartiality, and that any human system or order which interferes with this impartiality is contrary to the will of the Supreme Wisdom and Love. Is not this a kind of religion, and a very good kind? Do we not instinctively recognize a Divine authority in its voice when it says: "Whatsoever ye would that men should do unto you, do ye even so unto them"?

But in its practical operation in everyday affairs this spirit is not always conscious of its deep origin. It is not usually expressed in terms of religion, any more than an ordinary weighing-machine is inscribed with the formula of gravitation. It appears simply as the wish to conduct trade with just weights and measures, to live in a State which affords equal protection and opportunity to all its citizens, to play a game in which the rules are the same for every player, and a good stroke counts, no matter who makes it.

The Anglo-Saxon race has fallen into the habit of claiming this spirit of fair play as its own peculiar property. The claim does not illustrate the quality which it asserts. Certainly no one can defend the proposition that the growth of this spirit in America was due exclusively, or even chiefly, to English influence. It was in New England and in Virginia that ecclesiastical intolerance and social exclusiveness were most developed. In the middle colonies like New York, Pennsylvania, and Delaware, where the proportion of colonists from Holland, France, and Germany was much larger, a more liberal and tolerant spirit prevailed.

But, after all, it must be acknowledged that in the beginning there was no part of America where the spirit of self-reliance really carried with it that necessary complement,—the spirit of fair play. This was a thing of much slower growth. Indeed, it was not until the American people, passionately desiring self-rule, were brought into straits where they needed the help of every man to fight for independence, that they began to feel the right of every man to share equally in the benefits and privileges of that self-rule.

I pass by the discussion of the reasons why this second trait in the soul of the people developed later than the first. I pass by the tempting opportunity to describe the absurd pretensions of colonial aristocracy. I pass by the familiar theme of the inflexible prejudices of Puritan theocracy, which led men to interpret liberty of conscience as the right to practise their own form of worship and to persecute all others. I pass by the picturesque and neglected spectacle of the violence of the mobs which shouted for liberty—a violence which reminds one of the saying of Rivarol that "the crowd never believes that it has liberty until it attacks the liberties of others." All this I pass by for want of time, and come at once to the classic utterance of the spirit of fair play in America—I mean the Declaration of Independence.

If I must apologize for discussing a document so familiar, it is because familiarity, not being illuminated by intelligence, has bred in these latter days a certain kind of contempt. A false interpretation has led the enthusiastic admirers of the Declaration of Independence to complain that it has been abandoned, and its scornful despisers to say that it ought to be abandoned. The Declaration, in fact, has been as variously and as absurdly explained as the writings of St. Paul, of whom a French critic said that "the only man of the second century who understood St. Paul was Marcion, and he *mis*understood him."

Take the famous sentence from the beginning of that document. "We hold these truths to be self-evident; that all men are created equal; that they are endowed by their Creator with certain inalienable rights; that among these are life, liberty, and the pursuit of happiness; that to secure these rights, governments are instituted among men, deriving their just powers from the consent of the governed; that whenever any form of government becomes destructive of these ends, it is the right of the people to alter or to abolish it, and to institute a new form of government, laying its foundations on such principles and organizing its power in such form as to them shall seem most likely to effect their safety and happiness."

Now what have we here? A defence of revolution, no doubt, but not a sweeping and unqualified defence. It is carefully guarded and limited by the condition that revolution is justified only when government becomes destructive of its own ends,—the security and the happiness of the people.

And what have we here in the way of political doctrine? An assertion of the common rights of man as derived from his Creator, no doubt, and an implication that the specific prerogatives of rulers are not of divine origin. But there is no denial that the institution of government among men has a divine sanction. On the contrary, such a sanction is distinctly implied in the statement that government is necessary for the security of rights divinely given. There is no assertion of the divinity or even the superiority of any particular form of government, republican or democratic. On the contrary, "just powers" are recognized as derivable from the consent of the people. According to this view, a happy and consenting people under George III or Louis XVI would be as rightly and lawfully governed as a happy people under a congress and a president.

And what have we here in the way of social theory? An assertion of equality, no doubt, and a very flat-footed and peremptory assertion. "All men are created equal." But equal in what? In strength, in ability, in influence, in possessions. Not a word of it. The assertion of such a thing in an assembly which contained men as different as George Washington, with his lofty stature and rich estate, and Samuel Adams, for whose unimpressive person his friends were sometimes obliged to supply lodging and raiment, would have been a palpable absurdity.

"But," says Professor Wendell, "the Declaration only asserts that men are created equal, not that they must remain so." Not at all. It implies that what equality exists by creation ought to remain by protection. It is, and ought to be, inalienable.

But what is that equality? Not of person; for that would be to say that all men are alike, which is evidently false. Not of property; for that would be to say that all men are on a level, which never has been true, and, whether it is desirable or not, probably never will be true. The equality which is asserted among men refers simply to the rights which are common to men: life, liberty, and the pursuit of happiness. Here government must make no distinctions, no exceptions. Here the social order must impose no arbitrary and unequal deprivations and barriers. The life of all is equally sacred, the liberty of all must be equally secure, in order that the right of all to pursue happiness may be equally open.

Equality of opportunity: that is the proposition of the Declaration of Independence. And when you come to look at it closely, it does not seem at all unreasonable. For it proposes no alteration in the laws of the universe,—only a principle to be observed in human legislation. It predicts no Utopia of universal prosperity,—only a common adventure of equal risks and hopes. It has not the accent of that phrase, "Liberty, equality, fraternity, or death," which Chamfort translated so neatly, "Be my brother or I will kill you." It proceeds rather upon the assumption that fraternity already exists. It says, "We are brothers; therefore let us deal squarely with one another." It is, in fact, nothing more and nothing less than the voice of the spirit of fair play speaking gravely of the deepest interests of man. Here, in this game of life, it says, as we play it in America, the rules shall be the same for all. The penalties shall be the same for all. The prizes, so far as we can make it so, shall be open to all. And let the best man win.

This, so far as I can see it, or feel it, or comprehend it, is the sum total of democracy in America.

It is not an abstract theory of universal suffrage and the infallibility of the majority. For, as a matter of fact, universal suffrage never has existed in the United States and does not exist to-day. Each State has the right to fix its own conditions of suffrage. It may require a property qualification; and in the past many States imposed this condition. It may require an educational qualification; and to-day some States are imposing this condition. It may exclude the Chinese; and California, Oregon, and Nevada make this exclusion. It may admit only natives and foreigners who have been naturalized, as the majority of the States do. It may admit also foreigners who have merely declared their intention of becoming naturalized, as eleven of the States do. It may permit only men to vote, or it may expressly grant the suffrage to every citizen, male or female, as Idaho, Wyoming, Colorado, and Utah do. The only thing that the law of the nation says upon the subject is that when citizenship is established, the right to vote shall not be denied or abridged on account of race, colour, or previous condition of servitude.

It is entirely possible, therefore, that within this condition, suffrage should expand or contract in the United States according to the will of the people. Woman suffrage might come in next year without the change of a word in the Constitution. All that would be necessary would be a change in the mind of the women, the majority of whom at present do not want to vote, and would not do it if you paid them. On the other hand, educational and property qualifications might be proposed which would reduce the suffrage by a quarter or a third; but this, again, is not likely to happen. The point is that suffrage in America is not regarded as a universal and inalienable human right, but as a political privilege granted on the ground of fair play in order to make the rights of the people more secure.

The undeniable tendency has been to widen the suffrage; for Americans, as a rule, have a large confidence in the reasonableness of human nature, and believe that public opinion, properly and deliberately ascertained, will prove to be a wise and safe guide. But they recognize that a popular election may not always represent public opinion, that a people, like an individual, may and probably will need time to arrive at the best thought, the wisest counsel.

President Grover Cleveland, a confirmed and inflexible Democrat, but not an obstreperous or flamboyant one, often said to me, "You can trust the best judgment of the rank and file, but you cannot always reach that best judgment in a hurry." James Russell Lowell said pretty much the same thing: "An appeal to the reason of the people has never been known to fail in the long run." *The long run*,—that is the needful thing in the successful working of popular suffrage. And that the Americans have tried to gain by the division and distribution of powers, by the interposition of checks and delays, by lodging extraordinary privileges of veto in the hands of governors of States, and of the President of the United States. In short, by making swift action difficult and sudden action impossible, they have sought to secure fair play, even from the crowd, for every man and every interest.

There are some of us who think that this might have been done more easily and more certainly if the bounds of suffrage had not been made so wide. We doubt, for example, whether a group of day-labourers coming from Italy with their *padrone* are really protected in their natural rights by having the privilege of a vote before they can understand the language of the land in which they cast it. So far from being a protection, it seems to us like a danger. It exposes them to the seductions of the demagogue and to the control of the boss.

The suffrage of the ignorant is like a diamond hung round the neck of a little child who is sent out into the street: an invitation to robbers. It is like a stick of dynamite in the hands of a foolish boy: a prophecy of explosion.

There are some of us who think that "coming of age" might be measured by intelligence as well as by years; that it would be easier to get at the mind of the people if the vote were cast by the people who have minds; that a popular election would come nearer to representing public opinion if there were some way of sifting out at least a considerable part of those electors who can neither read nor write, nor understand the Constitution under which they are voting.

But whatever may be the thoughts and wishes of the more conservative Americans upon this subject, two things are certain. One is that the privilege of voting is a thing which is easy to give away and very hard to take back. The other sure thing is that the Spirit of America will never consent to any restriction of the suffrage which rests upon artificial distinctions, or seems to create ranks and orders and estates within the body politic. If any conditions are imposed, they must be the same for all. If the privilege should be in any way narrowed, it must still be open alike to all who will make the necessary effort to attain it. This is fair play; and this, so far as the suffrage and popular sovereignty are concerned, is what American democracy means. Not that every man shall count alike in the affairs of state, but that every man shall have an equal chance to make himself count for what he is worth.

Mark you, I do not say that this result has been fully accomplished in the United States. The machinery of parties interferes with it. The presentation of men and of measures from a purely partisan point of view interferes with it. In any national election it is reasonably sure that either the Republican party or the Democratic party will win. The policies and the candidates of both have been determined in committee or caucus, by processes which the ordinary citizen does not understand and cannot touch. But what if he does not like the results on either side? What if neither party seems to him clear or consistent or satisfactory? Still he must go with one or the other, or else be content to assert his individuality and lose his electoral efficiency by going in with one of the three or four little parties which stand for moral protest, or intellectual whim, or political vagary, without any possible chance of carrying the election.

A thoughtful man sometimes feels as if he were almost helpless amid the intricacies of the system by which his opinion on national affairs is asked. He sits with his vote in his hand as if it were some strange and antiquated instrument, and says to himself, "Now what, in heaven's name, am I going to do with this?"

In the large cities, especially, this sense of impotence is likely to trouble the intelligent and conscientious American. For here a species of man has developed called the *Boss*, who takes possession of the political machinery and uses it for his own purposes. He controls the party through a faction, and the faction through a gang, and the gang through a ring, and the ring by his own will, which is usually neither sweet nor savoury. He virtually owns the public franchises, the public offices, the public payroll. Like Rob Roy or Robin Hood, he takes tribute from the rich and distributes it to the poor,—for a consideration; namely, their personal loyalty to him. He leads his followers to the polls as a feudal chief led his retainers to battle. And the men whom he has chosen, the policies which he approves, are the ones that win.

What does this mean? The downfall of democracy? No; only the human weakness of the system in which democracy has sought to reach its ends; only the failure in duty, in many cases, of the very men who ought to have watched over the system in order to prevent its corruption.

It is because good men in America too often neglect politics that bad men sometimes control them. And, after all, when the evil goes far enough, it secretes its own remedy,—popular discontent, a reform movement, a peaceful revolution. The way is open. Speech is free. There is no need of pikes and barricades and firebrands. There is a more powerful weapon in every man's hand. Persuade him to use it for his own good. Combine the forces of intelligence and conscience, and the city which sees its own interest will find out how to secure it.

But the trouble, with such a mass of voters, is to produce this awakening, to secure this combination of better forces. It is a trouble which Americans often feel deeply, and of which they sometimes complain bitterly. But after all, if you can get down to the bottom of their minds, you will find that they would rather take their trouble in this form than in any other. They feel that there is something wholesome and bracing in the idea that people must want good government before they can get it. And for the sake of this they are willing, upon the whole, and except during intervals, to give that eternal vigilance which is the price of fair play.

It is not, however, of democracy as it has taken shape in political forms that I would speak; but rather of democracy as a spirit, a sentiment existing in the soul of the American people. The root of it is the feeling that the openings of life, so far as they are under human control, ought to be equal for all. The world may be like a house of many stories, some higher, some lower. But there shall be no locked doors between those stories. Every stairway shall be unbarred. Every man shall have his chance to rise. Every man shall be free to pursue his happiness, and protected in the enjoyment of his liberty, and secure in the possession of his life, so far as he does not interfere with others in the same rights.

This does not mean that all shall be treated alike, shall receive the same rewards. For, as Plato says, "The essence of equality lies in treating unequal things unequally." But it means what the first Napoleon called *la carrière ouverte aux talents*. Nay, it means a little more than that. For it goes beyond the talents, to the mediocrities, to the inefficiencies, and takes them into its just and humane and unprejudiced account. It means what President Roosevelt meant when he spoke of *"the square deal for everybody."* The soul of the American people answered to his words because he had expressed one of their dominant ideals.

You must not imagine that I propose to claim that this ideal has been perfectly realized in America. It is not true that every man gets justice there. It is not true that none are oppressed or unfairly treated. It is not true that every one finds the particular stairway which he wishes to climb open and unencumbered. But where is any ideal perfectly realized except in heaven and in the writings of female novelists? It is of the real desire and purpose, the good intention, the aim and temper of the American people, that I speak. And here I say, without doubt, the spirit of fair play has been, and still is, one of the creative and controlling factors of America.

If you should ask me for the best evidence to support this statement, I should at once name the Constitution and the Supreme Court of the United States. Here is an original institution, created and established by the people at the very birth of the nation, peculiar in its character and functions, I believe, to America, and embodying in visible form the spirit of fair play.

The laws under which a man must live in America are of three kinds. There is first the common law, which prevails in all the States except Louisiana, which is still under the Napoleonic Code. The common law, inherited from England, is contained in the mass of decisions and precedents handed down by the duly established courts from generation to generation. It is supposed to cover the principles which are likely to arise in almost all cases. But when a new principle appears, the judge must decide it according to his conscience and create the legal right.

The second source of law is found in statutes of the United States enacted by Congress, in the constitutions of the different States, and in the statutes enacted by the State legislatures. Here we have definite rules and regulations, not arising out of differences or disputes between individuals, but framed on general principles, and intended to cover all cases that may arise under them.

The third source of law is the Constitution of the United States, which is supreme and sovereign over all other laws. It is the enactment of the whole people. Congress did not create it. It created Congress. No legislation, whether of a State or of the nation, can impair or contravene its authority. It can only be changed by the same power which made it,—the people of the United States, expressing their will, first through a two-thirds majority of the national House and Senate, and then directly through the vote of three-fourths of the forty-six States.

Any statute which conflicts with the Constitution is invalid. Any State constitution which fails to conform to it is, in so far forth, non-existent. Any judicial decision which contradicts it is of no binding force. Over all the complexities of legislation and the perplexities of politics in America stands this law above the laws, this ultimate guarantee of fair play.

The thing to be noted in the Constitution is this: brief as it is for the creative document of a great nation, it contains an ample *Bill of Rights*, protecting every man alike. The Constitution, as originally framed in 1787, had omitted to do this fully, though it prohibited the States from passing any law to impair the validity of contracts, from suspending the writ of habeas corpus in time of peace, and from other things contrary to the spirit of fair play. But it was evident at once that the Constitution would not be ratified by a sufficient number of the States unless it went much farther. Massachusetts voiced the Spirit of America in presenting a series of amendments covering the ground of equal dealing with all men in the matters most essential to individual freedom and security. In 1790 these amendments, numbered from I to X, were passed by Congress, and in 1791 they became part of the Constitution.

What do they do? They guarantee religious liberty, freedom of speech and of the press, and the right of popular assembly and petition. They protect every man, in time of peace, from criminal indictment except by a grand jury, from secret trial, from compulsion to testify against himself, from being tried again for an offence of which he has been once acquitted, and from the requisition of excessive bail and the infliction of cruel or unusual punishments. They guarantee to him the right to be tried by an impartial jury of his peers and neighbours in criminal cases and in all suits under common law when the amount in controversy exceeds twenty dollars in value. They protect his house from search except under legal and specific warrant, and his property from appropriation for public use without just compensation. They assure him that he shall not be deprived of life, liberty, or property without due process of law.

The remarkable thing about these provisions for fair play is not so much their nature as the place where they are put. In England there is a Bill of Rights, embodied in various enactments, which covers pretty much the same ground. But these, as Mr. James Bryce says, "are merely ordinary laws, which could be repealed by Parliament at any moment in exactly the same way as it can repeal a highway act or lower the duty on tobacco." But in America they are placed upon a secure and lofty foundation, they are lifted above the passing storms of party politics. No State can touch them. No act of Congress can touch them. They belong to the law above laws.

Nor is this all. A supreme tribunal, coördinate with the national executive and legislature, independent and final in its action, is created by the Constitution itself to interpret and apply this supreme law. The nine judges who compose this court are chosen from the highest ranks of the legal profession, appointed by the President, and confirmed by the Senate. They hold office for life. Their court room is in the centre of the national Capitol, between the wings appropriated to the Senate and the House.

It is to that quiet chamber, so rich, so noble in its dignity and simplicity, so free from pomp and ostentation, so remote from turmoil and confusion, so filled with the tranquil glory of intelligence and conscience, so eloquent of confidence in the power of justice to vindicate itself,—it is to that room that I would take a foreigner who asked me why I believe that democracy in America has the promise of endurance. Those nine men, in their black judicial robes (the only officials of the nation who have from the beginning worn a uniform of office), are the symbols of the American conscience offering the ultimate guarantee of fair play. To them every case in law and equity arising under the Constitution, treaties and laws of the United States, every case of admiralty and marine jurisdiction, every case between citizens of different States, or between two States, every case in which the United States itself is a party, may be brought for final decision. For more than a hundred years this court has discharged its high functions without a suspicion of corruption or a shadow of reproach.

Twenty-one times it has annulled the action of Congress and declared it *ultra vires*. More than two hundred times it has found that State statutes were contrary to the Constitution and therefore practically non-existent. And these decisions are not made in the abstract, on theory, but in the concrete, on actual cases when the principle of fair play under the Constitution is at stake.

Let me illustrate this. In 1894 a law was passed by Congress taxing all incomes over a certain sum at certain rates. This was, in effect, not a tax based proportionally upon population, but a special tax upon a part of the population. It was also a direct tax levied by the national legislature. There was no necessity of discussing the abstract question of the wisdom or righteousness of such taxation. The only question was whether it was fair play under the Constitution. A citizen of New York refused to pay the tax; the case was brought to the Supreme Court and argued by Mr. Choate, the late American Ambassador to Great Britain. The court held that Congress had no power to impose such a tax, because the Constitution forbids that body to lay any direct tax, "unless in proportion to the census." By this one decision the income-tax law became null, as if it had never been.

Again, a certain citizen had obtained from the State of Georgia a grant of land upon certain terms. This grant was subsequently repealed by the State by a general statute. A case arose out of the conveyance of this land by a deed and covenant, and was carried to the Supreme Court. The court held that the statute of the State which took the citizen's land away from him was null, because it "impaired the obligation of a contract," which the Constitution expressly forbids.

Again, in 1890, Congress passed a measure commonly called the Sherman Anti-Trust Act, declaring "every contract, combination in the form of trusts or otherwise, or conspiracy in restraint of trade or commerce among the several States" to be illegal. This was undoubtedly intended to prevent the merger of railroads and manufacturing concerns into gigantic trusts with monopolistic powers. The American spirit has always understood liberty as including the right of the citizen to be free in the enjoyment of all his faculties, to live and work where he will, and in so doing to move freely from State to State. So far as the trusts were combinations in restraint of this right, the statute properly declared them illegal, and the Supreme Court so interpreted and applied it. But it soon became evident that combinations of labour might restrain trade just as much as combinations of capital. A strike or a boycott might paralyze an industry or stop a railroad. The Supreme Court did not hesitate to apply the same rule to the employees as to the employers. It held that a combination whose professed object is to arrest the operation of railroads whose lines extend from a great city into adjoining States until such roads accede to certain demands made upon them, whether such demands are in themselves reasonable or unreasonable, just or unjust, is certainly an unlawful conspiracy in restraint of commerce among the States.

Again and again the Supreme Court has interfered to prevent citizens of all the States from being deprived by the action of any State of those liberties which belong to them in common. Again and again its decisions have expressed and illustrated the fundamental American conviction which is summed up in the strong words of Justice Bradley: "The right to follow any of the common occupations of life is an inalienable right."

I have not spoken of the other federal courts and of the general machinery of justice in the United States, because there is not time to do so. If it were possible to characterize the general tendency in a sentence, I would say that it lays the primary emphasis on the protection of rights, and the secondary emphasis on the punishment of offences. Looking at the processes of justice from the outside, and describing things by their appearance, one might say that in many parts of the continent of Europe an accused man looks guilty till he is proved innocent; in America he looks innocent until his guilt is established.

The American tendency has its serious drawbacks,—legal delays, failures to convict, immunity of criminals, and so on. These are unpleasant and dangerous things. Yet, after all, when the thoughtful American looks at his country quietly and soberly he feels that a fundamental sense of justice prevails there not only in the courts but among the people. The exceptions are glaring, but they are still exceptions. And when he remembers the immense and inevitable perils of a republic, he reassures himself by considering the past history and the present power of the Supreme Court, that great bulwark against official encroachment, legislative tyranny, and mobocracy,—that grave and majestic symbol of the spirit of fair play. A republic with such an institution at the centre of its national conscience has at least one instrument of protection against the dangers which lurk in the periphery of its own passions.

If you should ask me for a second illustration of the spirit of fair play in America, I should name religious liberty and the peaceful independence of the churches within the state. I do not call it the "Separation of Church and State," because I fear that in France the phrase might carry a false meaning. It might convey the impression of a forcible rupture, or even a feeling of hostility, between the government and the religious bodies. Nothing of that kind exists in America. The state extends a firm and friendly protection to the adherents of all forms of religious belief or unbelief, defending all alike in their persons, in the possession of their property, and in their chosen method of pursuing happiness, whether in this world or in the next. It requires only that they shall not practise as a part of their cult anything contrary to public morality, such as polygamy, or physical cruelty, or neglect of children. Otherwise they are all free to follow the dictates of conscience in worshipping or in not worshipping, and in so doing they are under the shield of government.

This is guaranteed not only by the Constitution of the United States, but also by the separate State constitutions, so far as I know, without exception. Moreover, the general confidence and good-will of the state towards the churches is shown in many ways. Property used for religious purposes is exempted from taxation,—doubtless on the ground that these purposes are likely to promote good citizenship and orderly living. Religious marriage is recognized, but not required; and the act of a minister of any creed is, in this particular, as valid and binding as if he were a magistrate. But such marriages must be witnessed and registered according to law, and no church can annul them. It is the common practice to open sessions of the legislature, national and State, with an act of prayer; but participation in this act is voluntary. The President, according to ancient custom, appoints an annual day of national thanksgiving in the month of November, and his proclamation to this effect is repeated by the governors of the different States. But here, again, it is a proclamation of liberty. The people are simply recommended to assemble in their various places of worship, and to give thanks according to their conscience and faith.

The laws against blasphemy and against the disturbance of public worship which exist in most of the States offer an equal protection to a Jewish synagogue, a Catholic cathedral, a Buddhist temple, a Protestant church, and a Quaker meeting-house; and no citizen is under any compulsion to enter any one of these buildings, or to pay a penny of taxation for their support. Each religious organization regulates its own affairs and controls its own property. In cases of dispute arising within a church the civil law has decided, again and again, that the rule and constitution of the church itself shall prevail.

But what of the religious bodies which exist under this system? Do not imagine that they are small, feeble, or insignificant; that they are content to be merely tolerated; that they feel themselves in any way impotent or slighted. They include the large majority of the American people. Twelve millions are adherents of the Catholic Church. The adherents of the Protestant churches are estimated to number between forty and fifty millions. But neither as a whole, nor in any of their separate organizations, do the religious people of America feel that they are deprived of any real rights or robbed of any just powers.

It is true that the different churches are sometimes very jealous of one another. But bad as that may be for them, from a political point of view it is rather a safeguard.

It is true that ecclesiastics sometimes have dreams, and perhaps schemes, which look towards the obtaining of special privileges or powers for their own organization. But that is because ecclesiastics are human and fallible. In the main, you may say with confidence that there is no party or sect in America that has the slightest wish to see church and state united, or even entangled. The American people are content and happy that religion should be free and independent. And this contentment arises from three causes.

First, religious liberty has come naturally, peacefully, in a moderate and friendly temper, with consideration for the conscience and the rights of all, and at the same time, if I mistake not, with a general recognition that the essence of religion, personal faith in a spiritual life and a Divine law, is a purifying, strengthening, elevating factor in human society.

Second, the churches have prospered in freedom; they are well-to-do, they are active, they are able to erect fine edifices, to support their clergy, to carry on benevolent and missionary enterprises on an immense scale, costing many millions of dollars every year. The voluntary system has its great disadvantages and drawbacks,—its perils, even. But upon the whole, religious people in America, Catholics, Protestants, and Jews alike, feel that these are more than counterbalanced by the devotion which is begotten and nourished by the very act of making gifts and sacrifices, and by the sober strength which comes into a man's faith when he is called to support it by his works.

Men value what they pay for. But this is true only when they pay for what they really want.

Third, and chiefly, religious liberty commends itself to the Americans because they feel that it is the very highest kind of fair play. That a man should have freedom in the affairs of his soul is certainly most vital to his pursuit of happiness. The noble example of tolerance which was set to the American colonies by the Quakers of Pennsylvania, the Baptists of Rhode Island, and the Catholics of Maryland, prevailed slowly but surely over the opposite example of the Puritans of Massachusetts and the Anglicans of Virginia. The saying of William of Orange, "Conscience is God's province," has become one of the watchwords of America.

In a country which, as a matter of fact, is predominantly Christian and Protestant, there is neither establishment nor proscription of any form of faith. In the President's cabinet (1908) I personally know a Jew, a Catholic, a Presbyterian, an Episcopalian, and a Methodist. The President himself is a member of one of the smallest denominations in the country, the Dutch Reformed.

Nor is unfaith penalized or persecuted. A recent writer on America has said that "an avowed atheist is not received in any social circles above that of the ordinary saloon." Well, an atheist avowed in definite and unmistakable terms, a man who positively affirms that there is no God, is a very difficult person to find in this world of mystery. But a positivist, a free-thinker, a Voltairean, a sceptic, an agnostic, an antisupernaturalist of any kind, has the same rights and privileges as any other man. In America, if his life is clean and his manners decent, he goes everywhere. You may meet him in the best clubs, and in social circles which are at the farthest remove from the saloon. This is not because people like his opinions, but because they feel he is entitled to form them for himself. They take it for granted that it is as impossible to correct unbelief by earthly penalties as it is to deprive faith of its heavenly rewards.

I do not say that this is the right attitude, the only reasonable attitude. I do not wish to persuade any one to adopt it. I say only that it is the characteristic attitude of the Americans, and that sincerely religious people hold it, in the Catholic Church and in the Protestant Church. It may be that the spirit of fair play has blinded them. It may be that it has enlightened them. Be that as it may, they have passed beyond the point of demanding freedom of conscience for themselves to that of conceding it to others. And in this they think that they are acting in accordance with the Divine will and example.

An anecdote will illustrate this attitude better than many paragraphs of explanation. In the older American colleges, which were independent of state control, the original course of study was uniform and prescribed, and chapel services were held which the students were required to attend. Elective studies came in. The oldest of the universities made attendance at chapel voluntary. "I understand," said a critic to the president of the university, "that you have made God an elective in your college." The President thought for a moment. "No," said he, "we understand that He has made Himself elective everywhere."

There are certain singular limitations in the spirit of fair play in America of which I must say a word in order to play fair. Chief among these is the way in which the people of the colonies and of the United States dealt for many years with the races which have not a white skin.

The American Indians, in the seventeenth and eighteenth centuries, undoubtedly sinned as much as they were sinned against. They were treacherous, implacable, unspeakably cruel, horribly bloodthirsty. It is no wonder that the colonists regarded them as devils. It is no wonder that the feeling of mistrust and resentment persisted from one generation to another. But the strange thing is that when the Indians were subjugated and for the most part pacified, America still treated them from a hostile and alien point of view, denied them the rights of citizenship, took their property from them, and made it very difficult for them to pursue happiness in any reasonable form. For many years this treatment continued. It was so glaring that a book was written which described the Indian policy of the United States, not altogether unjustly, as *A Century of Dishonor*. Today all this is changed. The scattered and diminished remnants of the red men are admitted to citizenship if they wish it, and protected in their rights, and private benevolence vies with government in seeking to better their condition.

The African race, introduced into America for industrial reasons, multiplied more rapidly there than in its native home, and soon became a large factor in the population. But it was regarded and treated from a point of view totally different from that which controlled the treatment of the white factors. It did not share in the rights enumerated in the Declaration of Independence. It was an object of commerce, a source of wealth, a necessity of agriculture. The system of domestic slavery held practically all of the negroes in bondage (in spite of the fact that the Northern States abandoned it, and many of the best men in the South disliked it and protested against it) until the third quarter of the nineteenth century. It was approved, or at least tolerated, by the majority of the people until the Civil War did away with it. It has left as a legacy of retribution the most difficult and dangerous problem of America,—perhaps the greatest and most perplexing problem that any nation has ever had to face.

Nine millions of negroes, largely ignorant and naturally ill-fitted for self-government, are domiciled in the midst of a white population which in some sections of the South they outnumber. How to rule, protect, and educate this body of coloured people; how to secure them in their civil rights without admitting them to a racial mixture—that is the problem.

The Oriental races, recently coming to America in increasing numbers, receive from the people a welcome which cannot be described as cordial. The exclusion of the Chinese from citizenship, and in some States from immigration, is but a small symptom of the general situation. If any considerable number of Burmese or East Indians or Japanese should come, the situation would be the same, and it would be intensified with the increase of the numbers. They would not find the Americans inclined to make an open career for the Oriental talents.

Understand, I am not now condemning this state of affairs, nor am I defending it. That is not my business. I am simply trying to describe it. How is it to be reconciled with the spirit of fair play? I do not know. Perhaps reconciliation is impossible. But a partial understanding of the facts is possible, if you take into account *the doctrine of inferior races*.

This doctrine is not held or defended by all Americans. Some on religious grounds, some on philosophic grounds, would deny it. But on the mass of the people it has a firm, though in part an unrecognized, hold. They believe—or perhaps feel would be a better word—that the white race has an innate superiority to the coloured races. From this doctrine they have proceeded to draw conclusions, and curiously enough they have put them in the form of fair play. The Indians were not to be admitted to citizenship because they were the wards of the nation. The negroes were better off under slavery because they were like children, needing control and protection. They must still be kept in social dependence and tutelage because they will be safer and happier so. The Orientals are not fit for a share in American citizenship, and they shall not be let in because they will simply give us another inferior race to be taken care of.

I do not propose to discuss the philosophical consistency of such arguments. It is difficult to imagine what place Rousseau would have found for them in his doctrine of the state of nature and the rights of man.

The truth is that the Spirit of America has never been profoundly impressed with the idea of philosophical consistency. The Republic finds herself face to face not with a theory but with a condition. It is the immense mass of the African population that creates the difficulty for America. She means to give equal civil rights to her nine million negroes. She does not mean to let the black blood mix with the white. Whatever social division may be necessary to prevent this immense and formidable adulteration must be maintained intact.

Here, it seems to me, is the supreme test which the Spirit of America has to meet. In a certain sense the problem appears insoluble because it involves an insoluble race. But precisely here, in the necessity of keeping the negro race distinct, and in the duty of giving it full opportunity for self-development, fair play may find the occasion for a most notable and noble triumph.

I have left but a moment in which to speak of the influence of the kind of democracy which exists in America upon social conditions. In a word: it has produced a society of natural divisions without closed partitions, a temper of independence which shows itself either as self-assertion or self-respect according to the quality of the man, and an atmosphere of large opportunity which promotes general good humour.

In America, as elsewhere, people who have tastes and capacities in common consort together. An uneducated man will not find himself at ease in the habitual society of learned men who talk principally about books. A poor man will not feel comfortable if he attempts to keep company with those whose wealth has led them to immerse themselves in costly amusements. This makes classes, if you like, ranks, if you choose to call them so.

Moreover you will find that certain occupations and achievements which men have generally regarded with respect confer a kind of social distinction in America. Men who have become eminent in the learned professions, or in the army or navy, or in the higher sort of politics; men who have won success in literature or the other fine arts; men who have done notable things of various kinds,—such persons are likely to know each other better and to be better known to the world than if they had done nothing. Furthermore there are families in which this kind of thing has gone on from generation to generation; and others in which inherited wealth, moderate or great, has opened the way to culture and refinement; and others in which newly acquired wealth has been used with generosity and dignity; and others in which the mere mass of money has created a noteworthy establishment. These various people, divided among themselves by their tastes, their opinions, and perhaps as much as anything else by their favourite recreations, find their way into the red book of *Who's Who*, into the blue book of the Social Register. Here, if you have an imaginative turn of mind, you may discover (and denounce, or applaud, or ridicule) the beginnings of an aristocracy.

But if you use that word, remember that it is an aristocracy without legal privilege or prerogative, without definite boundaries, and without any rule of primogeniture. Therefore it seems to exist in the midst of democracy without serious friction or hostility. The typical American does not feel injured by the fact that another man is richer, better known, more influential than himself, unless he believes that the eminence has been unfairly reached. He respects those who respect themselves and him. He is ready to meet the men who are above him without servility, and the men who are beneath him without patronage.

True, he is sometimes a little hazy about the precise definition of "above" and "beneath." His feeling that all the doors are open may lead him to act as if he had already passed through a good many of them. There is at times an "I-could-if-I-would" air about him which is rather disconcerting.

There are great differences among Americans, of course, in regard to manners, ranging all the way from the most banal formality to the most exquisite informality. But in general you may say that manners are taken rather lightly, too lightly, perhaps, because they are not regarded as very real things. Their value as a means of discipline is often forgotten. The average American will not blush very deeply over a social blunder; he will laugh at it as a mistake in a game. But to really hurt you, or to lower his own independence, would make him feel badly indeed.

The free-and-easy atmosphere of the streets, the shops, the hotels, all public places, always strikes the foreigner, and sometimes very uncomfortably. The conductor on the railway car will not touch his hat to you; but, on the other hand, he does not expect a fee from you. The workman on the street of whom you ask a question will answer you as an equal, but he will tell you what you want to know. In the country the tone of familiarity is even more marked. If you board for the summer with a Yankee farmer, you can see that he not only thinks himself as good as you are, but that he cultivates a slightly artificial pity for you as "city folks."

In American family life there is often an absence of restraint and deference, in school and college life a lack of discipline and subordination, which looks ugly, and probably is rather unwholesome. One sometimes regrets in America the want of those tokens of respect which are the outward and visible sign of an inward and spiritual grace.

But, on the other hand, there is probably more good feeling, friendliness, plain human kindness, running around loose in America than anywhere else in the world. The sense of the essential equality of manhood takes away much of the sting of the inequalities of fortune. The knowledge of the open door reduces the offence of the stairway. It is pleasant and wholesome to live with men who have a feeling of the dignity and worth of their own occupations.

Our letter-carrier at Princeton never made any difference in his treatment of my neighbour President Cleveland and myself. He was equally kind to both of us, and I may add equally cheerful in rendering little friendly services outside of his strict duty. My guides in the backwoods of Maine and the Adirondacks regard me as a comrade who curiously enough makes his living by writing books, but who also shows that he knows the real value of life by spending his vacation in the forest. As a matter of fact, they think much more of their own skill with the axe and paddle than of my supposed ability with the pen. They have not a touch of subservience in their manner or their talk. They do their work willingly. They carry their packs, and chop the wood, and spread the tents, and make the bed of green boughs. And then, at night, around the camp-fire, they smoke their pipes with me, and the question is, Who can tell the best story?

IV
WILL-POWER, WORK, AND WEALTH

The Spirit of America is best known in Europe by one of its qualities,—*energy*. This is supposed to be so vast, so abnormal, that it overwhelms and obliterates all other qualities, and acts almost as a blind force, driving the whole nation along the highroad of unremitting toil for the development of physical power and the accumulation of material wealth.

La vie intense—which is the polite French translation of "the strenuous life"—is regarded as the unanimous choice of the Americans, who are never happy unless they are doing something, and never satisfied until they have made a great deal of money. The current view in Europe considers them as a well-meaning people enslaved by their own restless activity, bound to the service of gigantic industries, and captive to the adoration of a golden idol. But curiously enough they are often supposed to be unconscious both of the slavery and of the idolatry; in weaving the shackles of industrious materialism they imagine themselves to be free and strong; in bowing down to the Almighty Dollar they ignorantly worship an unknown god.

This European view of American energy, and its inexplicable nature, and its terrible results, seems to have something of the fairy tale about it. It is like the story of a giant, dreadful, but not altogether convincing. It lacks discrimination. In one point, at least, it is palpably incorrect. And with that point I propose to begin a more careful, and perhaps a more sane, consideration of the whole subject.

It is evidently not true that America is ignorant of the dangers that accompany her immense development of energy and its application in such large measure to material ends. Only the other day I was reading a book by an American about his country, which paints the picture in colours as fierce and forms as flat as the most modern of French decadent painters would use.

The author says: "There stands America, engaged in this superb struggle to dominate Nature and put the elements into bondage to man. Involuntarily all talents apply themselves to material production. No wonder that men of science no longer study Nature for Nature's sake; they must perforce put her powers into harness; no wonder that professors no longer teach knowledge for the sake of knowledge; they must make their students efficient factors in the industrial world; no wonder that clergymen no longer preach repentance for the sake of the kingdom of heaven; they must turn churches into prosperous corporations, multiplying communicants and distributing Christmas presents by the gross. Industrial civilization has decreed that statesmanship shall consist of schemes to make the nation richer, that presidents shall be elected with a view to the stock-market, that literature shall keep close to the life of the average man, and that art shall become national by means of a protective tariff....

"The process of this civilization is simple: the industrial habit of thought moulds the opinion of the majority, which rolls along, abstract and impersonal, gathering bulk till its giant figure is selected as the national conscience. As in an ecclesiastical state of society decrees of a council become articles of private faith, and men die for homoöusion or election, so in America the opinions of the majority, once pronounced, become primary rules of conduct.... The central ethical doctrine of industrial thought is that material production is the chief duty of man."

The author goes on to show that the acceptance of this doctrine has produced in America "*conventional sentimentality*" in the emotional life, "*spiritual feebleness*" in the religious life, "*formlessness*" in the social life, "*self-deception*" in the political life, and a "slovenly" intelligence in all matters outside of business. "We accept sentimentality," he says, "because we do not stop to consider whether our emotional life is worth an infusion of blood and vigour, rather than because we have deliberately decided that it is not. We neglect religion, because we cannot spare time to think what religion means, rather than because we judge it only worth a conventional lip service. We think poetry effeminate, because we do not read it, rather than because we believe its effect injurious. We have been swept off our feet by the brilliant success of our industrial civilization; and, blinded by vanity, we enumerate the list of our exports, we measure the swelling tide of our national prosperity; but we do not stop even to repeat to ourselves the names of other things."

This rather sweeping indictment against a whole civilization reminds me of the way in which one of my students once defined rhetoric. "Rhetoric," said this candid youth, "is the art of using words so as to make statements which are not entirely correct look like truths which nobody can deny."

The description of America given by her sad and angry friend resembles one of those relentless portraits which are made by rustic photographers. The unmitigated sunlight does its worst through an unadjusted lens; and the result is a picture which is fearfully and wonderfully made. "It looks like her," you say, "it looks horribly like her. But thank God I never saw her look just like that."

No one can deny that the life of America has developed more rapidly and more fully on the industrial side than on any other. No one can deny that the larger part, if not the better part, of her energy and effort has gone into the physical conquest of nature and the transformation of natural resources into material wealth. No one can deny that this undue absorption in one side of life has resulted in a certain meagreness and thinness on other sides. No one can deny that the immense prosperity of America, and her extraordinary success in agriculture, manufactures, commerce, and finance have produced a swollen sense of importance, which makes the country peddler feel as if he deserved some credit for the $450,000,000 balance of foreign trade in favour of the United States in 1907, and the barber's apprentice congratulate himself that American wealth is reckoned at $116,000,000,000, nearly twice that of the next richest country in the world. This feeling is one that has its roots in human nature. The very cabin-boy on a monstrous ocean steamship is proud of its tonnage and speed.

But that this spirit is not universal nor exclusive, that there are some Americans who are not satisfied—who are even rather bitterly dissatisfied—with $116,000,000,000 as a statement of national achievement, the book from which I have quoted may be taken as a proof. There are still better proofs to be found, I think, in the earnestly warning voices which come from press and pulpit against the dangers of commercialism, and in the hundreds of thousands of noble lives which are freely consecrated to ideals in religion, in philanthropy, in the service of man's intellectual and moral needs. These services are ill-paid in America, as indeed they are everywhere, but there is no lack of men and women who are ready and glad to undertake them.

I was talking to a young man and woman the other day, both thoroughbred Americans, who had resolved to enter upon the adventure of matrimony together. The question was whether he should accept an opening in business with a fair outlook for making a fortune, or take a position as teacher in a school with a possible chance at best of earning a comfortable living. They asked my advice. I put the alternative as clearly as I could. On the one hand, a lot of money for doing work that was perfectly honest, but not at all congenial. On the other hand, small pay in the beginning, and no chance of ever receiving more than a modest competence for doing work that was rather hard but entirely congenial. They did not hesitate a moment. "We shall get more out of life," they said with one accord, "if our work makes us happy, than if we get big pay for doing what we do not love to do." They were not exceptional. They were typical of the best young Americans. The noteworthy thing is that both of them took for granted the necessity of *doing something* as long as they lived.

The notion of a state of idleness, either as a right or as a reward, never entered their blessed young minds.

In later lectures I shall speak of some of the larger evidences in education, in social effort, and in literature, which encourage the hope that the emotional life of America is not altogether a "conventional sentimentality," nor her spiritual life a complete "feebleness," nor her intelligence entirely "slovenly." But just now we have to consider the real reason and significance of the greater strength, the fuller development of the industrial life. Let us try to look at it clearly and logically. My wish is not to accuse, nor to defend, but first of all to understand.

The astonishing industrial advance of the United States, and the predominance of this motive in the national life, come from the third element in the spirit of America, *will-power*, that vital energy of nature which makes an ideal of activity and efficiency. "The man who does things" is the man whom the average American admires.

No doubt the original conditions of the nation's birth and growth were potent in directing this will-power, in transforming this energy into forces of a practical and material kind. A new land offered the opportunity, a wild land presented the necessity, a rich land held out the reward, to men who were eager to do something. But though the outward circumstances may have moulded and developed the energy, they did not create it.

Mexico and South America were new lands, wild lands, rich lands. They are not far inferior, if at all, to the United States in soil, climate, and natural resources. They presented the same kind of opportunity, necessity, and reward to their settlers and conquerors. Yet they have seen nothing like the same industrial advance. Why? There may be many reasons. But I am sure that the most important reasons lie in the soul of the people, and that one of them is the lack, in the republics of the South, of that strong and confident will-power which has made the Americans a nation of hard and quick workers.

This fondness for the active life, this impulse to "do things," this sense of value in the thing done, does not seem to be an affair of recent growth in America. It is an ancestral quality.

The men of the Revolution were almost all of them busy and laborious persons, whether they were rich or poor. Read the autobiography of Benjamin Franklin, and you will find that he was as proud of the fact that he was a good printer and that he invented a new kind of stove as of anything else in his career. One of his life mottoes under the head of industry is: "Lose no time; be always employed in something useful; cut off all unnecessary actions." Washington, retiring from his second term in the presidency, did not seek a well-earned ease, but turned at once to the active improvement of his estate. He was not only the richest man, he was one of the best practical farmers in America. His diary shows how willingly and steadily he rode his daily rounds, cultivated his crops, sought to improve the methods of agriculture and the condition and efficiency of his work-people. And this primarily not because he wished to add to his wealth,—for he was a childless man and a person of modest habits,—but because he felt "*il faut cultiver son jardin.*"

After the nation had defended its independence and consolidated its union, its first effort was to develop and extend its territory. It was little more than a string of widely separated settlements along the Atlantic coast. Some one has called it a country without an interior. The history of the pioneers who pushed over the mountains of the Blue Ridge and the Alleghanies, into the forests of Tennessee and Kentucky, into the valleys of the Ohio and the Mississippi, and so on to the broad rolling prairies of the West, is not without an interest to those who feel the essential romance of the human will in a world of intractable things. The transformation of the Indian's hunting trail into the highroad, with its train of creaking, white-topped wagons, and of the highroad into the railway, with its incessant, swift-rushing caravans of passengers and freight; the growth of enormous cities like Chicago and St. Louis in places that three generations ago were a habitation for wild geese and foxes; the harnessing of swift and mighty rivers to turn the wheels of innumerable factories; the passing of the Great American Desert, which once occupied the centre of our map, into the pasture-ground of countless flocks and herds, and the grain-field where the bread grows for many nations,—all this, happening in a hundred years, has an air of enchantment about it. What wonder that the American people have been fascinated, perhaps even a little intoxicated, by the effect of their own will-power?

In 1850 they were comparatively a poor people, with only $7,000,000,000 of national wealth, less than $308 *per capita*. In 1906 they had become a rich people, with $107,000,000,000 of national wealth, more than $1300 *per capita*. In 1850 they manufactured $1,000,000,000 worth of goods, in 1906 $14,000,000,000 worth. In 1850 they imported $173,000,000 worth of merchandise and exported $144,000,000 worth. In 1906 the figures had changed to $1,700,000,000 of merchandise exports and $1,200,000,000 of imports. That is to say, in one year America sold to other nations six dollars' worth *per capita* more than she needed to buy from them.

I use these figures, not because I find them particularly interesting or philosophically significant, but because the mere size of them illustrates, and perhaps explains, a point that is noteworthy in the development of will-power in the American people: and that is its characteristic spirit of *magnificence*. I take this word for want of a better, and employ it, according to its derivation, to signify the desire to do things on a large scale. This is a spirit which is growing everywhere in the modern civilized world. Everywhere, if I mistake not, quantity is taking precedence of quality in the popular thought. Everywhere men are carried away by the attraction of huge enterprises, immense combinations, enormous results. One reason is that Nature herself seems to have put a premium upon the mere mass of things. In the industrial world it appears as if Napoleon were right in his observation that "God is on the side of the big battalions." Another reason is the strange, almost hypnotic, effect that number has upon the human mind.

But while the spirit of "the large scale" is gaining all over the world, among the Americans it seems to be innate and most characteristic. Perhaps the very size of their country may have had something to do with this. The habit of dealing with land in terms of the square mile and the quarter-section, instead of in the terms of the *are* and the *hectare*; the subconscious effect of owning the longest river and the largest lakes in the world may have developed a half-humorous, half-serious sense of necessity for doing things magnificently in order to keep in proportion with the natural surroundings. A well-known American wit, who had a slight impediment in his speech, moved his residence from Baltimore to New York. "Do you make as many jokes here," asked a friend, "as you used to make in Baltimore?" "M-m-more!" he answered; "b-b-bigger town!"

To produce more corn and cotton than all the rest of the world together, to have a wheat crop which is more than double that of any other country; to mine a million tons of coal a year in excess of any rival; to double Germany's output of steel and iron and to treble Great Britain's output,—these are things which give the American spirit the sense of living up to its opportunities.

It likes to have the tallest buildings in the world. New York alone contains more than twenty-five architectural eruptions of more than twenty stories each. There is an edifice now completed which is 909 feet in height. One is planned which will be 1000 feet tall, 16 feet taller than the Eiffel Tower. This new building will not be merely to gratify (or to shock) the eye like the Parisian monument of magnificence in architecture. "The Eiffel Tower," says the American, "is not a real sky-scraper, *gratte-ciel*; it is only a sky-tickler, *chatouille-ciel*; nothing more than a *jeu d'esprit* which man has played with the law of gravitation. But our American tall building will be strictly for business, a serious affair, the office of a great life-insurance company." There is a single American factory which makes 1500 railway locomotives every year. There is a company for the manufacture of harvesting-machines in Chicago whose plant covers 140 acres, whose employees number 24,000, and whose products go all over the world.

Undoubtedly it was the desire to promote industrial development that led to the adoption of the protective tariff as an American policy. The people wanted to do things, to do all sorts of things, and to do them on a large scale. They were not satisfied to be merely farmers, or miners, or fishermen, or sailors, or lumbermen. They wished to exercise their energy in all possible ways, and to secure their prosperity by learning how to do everything necessary for themselves. They began to lay duties upon goods manufactured in Europe in order to make a better market at home for goods manufactured in America. "Protection of infant industries" was the idea that guided them. There have been occasional intervals when the other idea, that of liberty for needy consumers to buy in the cheapest market, has prevailed, and tariffs have been reduced. But in general the effort has been not only to raise a large part of the national income by duties on imports, but also to enhance the profits of native industries by putting a handicap on foreign competition.

There can be no question that the result has been to foster the weaker industries and make them strong, and actually to create some new fields for American energy to work in. For example, in 1891 there was not a pound of tin-plate made in the United States, and 1,000,000,000 pounds a year were imported. The McKinley tariff put on an import duty of 70 per cent. In 1901 only a little over 100,000,000 pounds of tin-plate were imported, and nearly 900,000,000 pounds were made in America. The same thing happened in the manufacture of watches. A duty of 25 per cent on the foreign article gave the native manufacturer a profit, encouraged the development of better machinery, and made the American watch tick busily around the world. Now (1908) the duty is 40 per cent *ad valorem*.

No one in the United States would deny these facts. No one, outside of academic circles, would call himself an absolute, unmitigated, and immediate free-trader. But a great many people, probably the majority of the Democratic party, and a considerable number in the Republican party, say to-day that many of the protective features of the tariff have largely accomplished their purpose and gone beyond it; that they have not only nourished weak industries, but have also overstimulated strong ones; that their continuance creates special privileges in the commercial world, raises the cost of the necessities of life to the poor man, tends to the promotion of gigantic trusts and monopolies, and encourages overproduction, with all its attendant evils enhanced by an artificially sustained market.

They ask why a ton of American steel rail should cost twenty-six or twenty-seven dollars in the country where it is made, and only twenty dollars in Europe. They inquire why a citizen of Chicago or St. Louis has to pay more for an American sewing-machine or clock than a citizen of Stockholm or Copenhagen pays for the same article. They say that a heavy burden has been laid upon the common people by a system of indirect taxation, adopted for a special purpose, and maintained long after that purpose has been fulfilled. They claim that for every dollar which this system yields to the national revenue it adds four or five dollars to the profits of the trusts and corporations. If they are cautious by temperament, they say that they are in favour of moderate tariff revision. If they are bold, they announce their adherence to the doctrine of "tariff for revenue only."

The extent to which these views have gained ground among the American people may be seen in the platforms of both political parties in the presidential contest of 1908. Both declare in favour of a reduction in the tariff. The Republicans are for continued protective duties, with revision of the schedules and the adoption of maximum and minimum rates, to be used in obtaining advantages from other nations. The Democrats are for placing products which are controlled by trusts on the free list; for lowering the duty upon all the necessaries of life at once; and for a gradual reduction of the schedules to a revenue basis. The Democrats are a shade more radical than the Republicans. But both sides are a little reserved, a little afraid to declare themselves frankly and unequivocally, a good deal inclined to make their first appeal to the American passion for industrial activity and prosperity.

Personally I should like to see this reserve vanish. I should like to see an out-and-out campaign on the protection which our industries need compared with that which they want and get. It would clear the air. It would be a campaign of education. I remember what the greatest iron-master of America—Mr. Andrew Carnegie—said to me in 1893 when I was travelling with him in Egypt. It was in the second term of Cleveland's administration, when the prospect of tariff reduction was imminent. I asked him if he was not afraid that the duty on steel would be reduced to a point that would ruin his business. "Not a bit," he answered, "and I have told the President so. The tariff was made for the protection of infant industries. But the steel business of America is not an infant. It is a giant. It can take care of itself." Since that time the United States Steel Corporation has been formed, with a capitalization of about fifteen hundred million dollars of bonds and stock, and the import duty on manufactured iron and steel is 45 per cent *ad valorem*.

Another effect of the direction of American energy to industrial affairs has been important not only to the United States but to all the nations of the world. I mean the powerful stimulus which it has given to invention. People with restless minds and a strong turn for business are always on the lookout for new things to do and new ways of doing them. The natural world seems to them like a treasure-house with locked doors which it is their duty and privilege to unlock. No sooner is a new force discovered than they want to slip a collar over it and put it to work. No sooner is a new machine made than they are anxious to improve it.

The same propensity makes a public ready to try new devices, and to adopt them promptly as soon as they prove useful. "Yankee notions" is a slang name that was once applied to all sorts of curious and novel trifles in a peddler's stock. But to-day there are a hundred Yankee notions without the use of which the world's work would go on much more slowly. The cotton-gin takes the seeds from seven thousand pounds of cotton in just the same time that a hand picker formerly needed to clean a pound and a half. An American harvesting-machine rolls through a wheat-field, mowing, threshing, and winnowing the wheat, and packing it in bags, faster than a score of hands could do the work. The steamboat, the sewing-machine, the electric telegraph, the type-writer, the telephone, the incandescent light,— these are some of the things with which American ingenuity and energy have been busy for the increase of man's efficiency and power in the world of matter. The mysterious force or fluid which Franklin first drew quietly to the earth with his little kite and his silken cord has been put to a score of tasks which Franklin never dreamed of. And in the problem of aerial navigation, which is now so much in the air everywhere, it looks as if American inventors might be the first to reach a practical solution.

I do not say that this indicates greatness. I say only that it shows the presence in the Spirit of America of a highly developed will-power, strong, active, restless, directed with intensity to practical affairs. The American inventor is not necessarily, nor primarily, a man who is out after money. He is hunting a different kind of game, and one which interests him far more deeply: a triumph over nature, a conquest of time or space, the training of a wild force, or the discovery of a new one. He likes money, of course. Most men do. But the thing that he most loves is to take a trick in man's long game with the obstinacy of matter.

Edison is a typical American in this. He has made money, to be sure; but very little in comparison with what other men have made out of his inventions. And what he gains by one experiment he is always ready to spend on another, to risk in a new adventure. His real reward lies in the sense of winning a little victory over this secretive world, of taking another step in the subjugation of things to the will of man.

There is probably no country where new inventions, labour-saving devices, improved machinery, are as readily welcomed and as quickly taken up as in America. The farmer wants the newest plough, the best reaper and mower. His wife must have a sewing-machine of the latest model; his daughter a pianola; his son an electric runabout or a motor-cycle. The factories are always throwing out old machinery and putting in new. The junk-heap is enormous. The waste looks frightful; and so it would be, if it were not directed to a purpose which in the end makes it a saving.

American cities are always in a state of transition. Good buildings are pulled down to make room for better ones. My wife says that "New York will be a delightful place to live in when it is finished." But it will never be finished. It is like Tennyson's description of the mystical city of Camelot:—

> "always building,
> Therefore never to be built at all."

But unlike Camelot, it is not built to music,—rather to an accompaniment of various and dreadful noise.

Even natural catastrophes which fall upon cities in America seem to be almost welcomed as an invitation to improve them. A fire laid the business portion of Baltimore in ashes a few years ago. Before the smoke had dispersed, the Baltimoreans were saying, "Now we can have wider streets and larger stores." An earthquake shook San Francisco to pieces. The people were stunned for a little while. Then they rubbed the dust out of their eyes, and said, "This time we shall know how to build better."

The high stimulation of will-power in America has had the effect of quickening the general pace of life to a rate that always astonishes and sometimes annoys the European visitor. The movement of things and people is rapid, incessant, bewildering. There is a rushing tide of life in the streets, a nervous tension in the air. Business is transacted with swift despatch and close attention. The preliminary compliments and courtesies are eliminated. Whether you want to buy a paper of pins, or a thousand shares of stock, it is done quickly. I remember that I once had to wait an hour in the Ottoman Bank at Damascus to get a thousand francs on my letter of credit. The courteous director gave me coffee and delightful talk. In New York the transaction would not have taken five minutes,—but there would have been no coffee nor conversation.

Of course the rate of speed varies considerably in different parts of the country. In the South it is much slower than in the North and the West. In the rural districts you will often find the old-fashioned virtues of delay and deliberation carried to an exasperating point of perfection. Even among the American cities there is a difference in the rapidity of the pulse of life. New

York and Chicago have the name of the swiftest towns. Philadelphia has a traditional reputation for a calm that borders on somnolence. "How many children have you?" some one asked a Chicagoan. "Four," was his answer; "three living, and one in Philadelphia."

I was reading only a few day ago an amusing description of the impression which the American *pas-redoublé* of existence made upon an amiable French observer, M. Hugues Le Roux, one of the lecturers who came to the United States on the Hyde foundation. He says:—

"Everywhere you see the signs of shopkeepers who promise to do a lot of things for you '*while you wait.*' The tailor will press your coat, the hatter will block your hat, the shoemaker will mend your shoe,—*while you wait.* At the barber shops the spectacle becomes irresistibly comic. The American throws himself back in an arm-chair to be shaved, while another artist cuts his hair; at the same time his two feet are stretched out to a bootblack, and his two hands are given up to a manicure....

"If 'Step lively' is the first exclamation that a foreigner hears on leaving the steamship, 'Quick' is the second. Everything here is quick. In the business quarter you read in the windows of the restaurants, as their only guarantee of culinary excellence, this alluring promise: 'Quick lunch!'...

"The American is born 'quick'; works 'quick'; eats 'quick'; decides 'quick'; gets rich 'quick'; and dies 'quick.' I will add that he is buried 'quick.' Funerals cross the city *au triple galop.*"

So far as it relates to the appearance of things, what the philosopher would call the phenomenal world, this is a good, though slightly exaggerated, description. I have never been so fortunate as to see a man getting a "shave" and a "hair-cut" at the same moment; and it seems a little difficult to understand precisely how these two operations could be performed simultaneously, unless the man wore a wig. But if it can be done, no doubt the Americans will learn to have it done that way. As for the hair-cutter, the manicure, and the bootblack, the combination of their services is already an accomplished fact, made possible by the kindness of nature in placing the head, the hands, and the feet at a convenient distance from one another. Even the Parisian barbers have taken advantage of this fact. They sell you a bottle of hair tonic at the same time.

It is true that the American moves rapidly. But if you should infer from these surface indications that he is always in a hurry, you would make a mistake. His fundamental philosophy is that you must be quick sometimes if you do not wish to be hurried always. You must condense, you must eliminate, you must save time on the little things in order that you may have more time for the larger things. He systematizes his correspondence, the labour of his office, all the details of his business, not for the sake of system, but for the sake of getting through with his work.

Over his desk hangs a printed motto: "This is my busy day." He does not like to arrive at the railway station fifteen minutes before the departure of his train, because he has something else that he would rather do with those fifteen minutes. He does not like to spend an hour in the barber-shop, because he wishes to get out to his country club in good time for a game of golf and a shower-bath afterward. He likes to have a full life, in which one thing connects with another promptly and neatly, without unnecessary intervals. His characteristic attitude is not that of a man in a hurry, but that of a man concentrated on the thing in hand in order to save time.

President Roosevelt has described this American trait in his familiar phrase, "the strenuous life." In a man of ardent and impetuous temperament it may seem at times to have an accent of overstrain. Yet this is doubtless more in appearance than in reality. There is probably no man in the world who has comfortably gotten through with more work and enjoyed more play than he has.

But evidently this American type of life has its great drawbacks and disadvantages. In eliminating the intervals it is likely to lose some of the music of existence. In laying such a heavy stress upon the value of action it is likely to overlook the part played by reflection, by meditation, by tranquil consideration in a sane and well-rounded character.

The critical faculty is not that in which Americans excel. By this I do not mean to say that they do not find fault. They do, and often with vigour and acerbity. But fault-finding is not criticism in the true sense of the word. Criticism is a disinterested effort to see things as they really are, to understand their causes, their relations, their effects. In this effort the French intelligence seems more at home, more penetrating, better balanced than the American.

Minds of the type of Sainte Beuve or Brunetière are not common, I suppose, even in France. But in America they are still more rare. Clear, intelligent, thoroughgoing, well-balanced critics are not much in evidence in the United States; first, because the genius of the country does not tend to produce them; and second, because the taste of the people does not incline to listen to them.

There is a spirit in the air which constantly cries, "Act, act!"

"Let us still be up and doing."

The gentle voice of that other spirit which whispers, "Consider, that thou mayest be wise," is often unheard or unheeded.

It is plain that the restless impulse to the active life, coming from the inward fountain of will-power, must make heavy drafts upon its source, and put a severe strain upon the channels by which it is conveyed. The nerves are worn and frayed by constant pressure. America is the country of young men, but many of them look old before their time. Nervous exhaustion is common. Neurasthenia, I believe, is called "the American disease."

Yet, curiously enough, it was in France that the best treatment of this disease was developed, and one of the most famous practitioners, Dr. Charcot, died, if I mistake not, of the complaint to the cure of which he had given his life. In spite of the fact that nervous disorders are common among Americans, they do not seem to lead to an unusual number of cases of mental wreck. I have been looking into the statistics of insanity. The latest figures that I have been able to find are as follows: In 1900 the United States had 106,500 insane persons in a population of 76,000,000. In 1896 Great Britain and Ireland had 128,800 in a population of 37,000,000. In 1884 France had 93,900 in a population of 40,000,000. That would make about 328 insane persons in 100,000 for Great Britain, 235 in every 100,000 for France, 143 in every 100,000 for America.

Nor does the wear and tear of American life, great as it may be, seem to kill people with extraordinary rapidity. As a matter of fact, M. Le Roux was led away by the allurements of his own style when he wrote that the American "dies quick." In 1900 the annual death-rate per 1000 in Austria was 25, in Italy 23, in Germany 22, in France 21, in Belgium 19, in Great Britain 18, and in the United States 17. In America the average age at death in 1890 was 31 years; in 1900 it was 35 years. Other things, such as climate, sanitation, hygiene, have to be taken into account in reading these figures. But after making all allowance for these things, the example of America does not indicate that an active, busy, quick-moving life is necessarily a short one. On the contrary, hard work seems to be wholesome. Employed energy favours longevity.

But what about the amount of pleasure, of real joy, of inward satisfaction that a man gets out of life? Who can make a general estimate in a matter which depends so much upon individual temperament? Certainly there are some deep and quiet springs of happiness which look as if they were in danger of being choked and lost, or at least which do not flow as fully and freely as one could wish, in America.

The tranquil pleasure of the household where parents and children meet in intimate, well-ordered, affectionate and graceful fellowship—the *foyer*, as the best French people understand and cherish it—is not as frequent in America as it might be, nor as it used to be. There are still many sweet and refreshing homes, to be sure. But "the home" as a national institution, the centre and the source of life, is being crowded out a little. Children as well as parents grow too busy for it.

Human intercourse, also, suffers from the lack of leisure, and detachment, and delight in the interchange of ideas. The average American is not silent. He talks freely and sometimes well, but he usually does it with a practical purpose. Political debate and business discussion are much more in his line than general conversation. Thus he too often misses what Montaigne and Samuel Johnson both called one of the chief joys of life,— "a good talk." I remember one morning, after a certain dinner in New York, an acquaintance who was one of the company met me, and said, "Do you know that we dined last night with thirty millions of dollars?" "Yes," I said, "and we had conversation to the amount of about thirty cents."

Popular recreations and amusements, pleasures of the simpler kind such as are shared by masses of people on public holidays, do not seem to afford as much relaxation and refreshment in America as they do in Germany or France. Children do not take as much part in them. There is an air of effort about them, as if the minds of the people were not quite free from care. The Englishman is said to take his pleasure sadly. The American is apt to take his strenuously.

Understand, in all this I am speaking in the most general way, and of impressions which can hardly be defined, and which certainly cannot be mathematically verified. I know very well that there are many exceptions to what I have been saying. There are plenty of quiet rooms in America, club-rooms, college-rooms, book-rooms, parlours, where you will find the best kind of talk. There are houses full of children who are both well-bred and happy. There are people who know how to play, with a free heart, not for the sake of winning, but for the pleasure of the game.

Yet I think it true that a strong will-power directed chiefly to industrial success has had a hardening effect upon the general tone of life. Unless you really love work for its own sake, you will not be very happy in America. The idea of a leisure class is not fully acclimatized there. Men take it for granted that there must be something useful for them to do in the world, even though they may not have to earn a living.

This brings me to the last point of which I wish to speak: the result of will-power and work in the production of wealth, and the real status of the Almighty Dollar in the United States.

The enormous increase of wealth has been accompanied by an extraordinary concentration of it in forms which make it more powerful and impressive. Moody's *Manual of Corporation Statistics* says that there are four hundred and forty large industrial, franchise, and transportation trusts, of an important and active character, with a floating capital of over twenty billion dollars. When we remember that each of these corporations is in the eye of the law a person, and is able to act as a person in financial, industrial, and political affairs, we begin to see the tremendous significance of the figures.

But we must remember also that the growth of individual fortunes and of family estates has been equally extraordinary. Millionnaires are no longer counted. It is the multi-millionnaires who hold the centre of the stage. The *New York World Almanac* gives a list of sixteen of these families of vast wealth, tracing the descent of their children and grandchildren with scrupulous care, as if for an *Almanach de Gotha*. I suppose that another list might be made twice as large,—three or four times as large,—who knows how large,—of people whose fortune runs up into the tens of millions.

These men have a vast power in American finance and industry, not only by the personal possession of money, but also through the control of the great trusts, railroads, banks, in which they have invested it. The names of many of them are familiar throughout the country. Their comings and goings, their doings, opinions, and tastes are set forth in the newspapers. Their houses, their establishments, in some cases are palatial; in other cases they are astonishingly plain and modest. But however that may be, the men themselves, as a class, are prominent, they are talked about, they hold the public attention.

What is the nature of this attention? Is it the culminating rite in the worship of the Almighty Dollar? No; it is an attention of curiosity, of natural interest, of critical consideration.

The dollar *per se* is no more almighty in America than it is anywhere else. It has just the same kind of power that the franc has in France, that the pound has in England: the power to buy the things that can be bought. There are foolish people in every country who worship money for its own sake. There are ambitious people in every country who worship money because they have an exaggerated idea of what it can buy. But the characteristic thing in the attitude of the Americans toward money is this: not that they adore the dollar, but that they admire the energy, the will-power, by which the dollar has been won.

They consider the multi-millionnaire much less as the possessor of an enormous fortune than as the successful leader of great enterprises in the world of affairs, a master of the steel industry, the head of a great railway system, the developer of the production of mineral oil, the organizer of large concerns which promote general prosperity. He represents to them achievement, force, courage, tireless will-power.

A man who is very rich merely by inheritance, who has no manifest share in the activities of the country, has quite a different place in their attention. They are entertained, or perhaps shocked, by his expenditures, but they regard him lightly.

It is the man who does things, and does them largely, in whom they take a serious interest. They are inclined, perhaps, to pardon him for things that ought not to be pardoned, because they feel so strongly the fascination of his potent will, his practical efficiency.

It is not the might of the dollar that impresses them, it is the might of the man who wins the dollar magnificently by the development of American industry.

This, I assure you, is the characteristic attitude of the typical American toward wealth. It does not confer a social status by itself in the United States any more than it does in England or in France. But it commands public attention by its relation to national will-power.

Of late there has come into this attention a new note of more searching inquiry, of sharper criticism, in regard to the use of great wealth.

Is it employed for generous and noble ends, for the building and endowment of hospitals, of public museums, libraries, and art galleries, for the support of schools and universities, for the education of the negro? Then the distributer is honoured.

Is it devoted even to some less popular purpose, like Egyptian excavations, or polar expeditions, or the endowment of some favourite study,—some object which the mass of the people do not quite understand, but which they vaguely recognize as having an ideal air? Then the donor is respected even by the people who wonder why he does that particular thing.

Is it merely hoarded, or used for selfish and extravagant luxury? Then the possessor is regarded with suspicion, with hostility, or with half-humorous contempt.

There is, in fact, as much difference in the comparative standing of multi-millionnaires in America as there is in the comparative standing of lawyers or politicians. Even in the same family, when a great fortune is divided, the heir who makes a good and fine use of the inheritance receives the tribute of affection and praise, while the heir who hoards it, or squanders it ignobly, receives only the tribute of notoriety,—which is quite a different thing. The power of discrimination has not been altogether blinded by the glitter of gold. The soul of the people in America accepts the law of the moral dividend which says *Richesse oblige*.

Here I might stop, were it not for the fact that still another factor is coming into the attitude of the American people toward great wealth, concentrated wealth. There is a growing apprehension that the will-power of one man may be so magnified and extended by the enormous accumulation of the results of his energy and skill as to interfere with the free exercise of the will-power of other men. There is a feeling that great trusts carry within themselves the temptation to industrial oppression, that the liberty of individual initiative may be threatened, that the private man may find himself in a kind of bondage to these immense and potent artificial personalities created by the law.

Beyond a doubt this feeling is spreading. Beyond a doubt it will lead to some peaceful effort to regulate and control the great corporations in their methods. And if that fails, what then? Probably an effort to make the concentration of large wealth in a few hands more difficult if not impossible. And if that fails, what then? Who knows? But I think it is not likely to be anything of the nature of communism.

The ruling passion of America is not equality, but personal freedom for every man to exercise his will-power under a system of self-reliance and fair play.

V
COMMON ORDER AND SOCIAL COÖPERATION

It is a little strange, and yet it seems to be true, that for a long time America was better understood by the French than by the English. This may be partly due to the fact that the French are more idealistic and more excitable than the English; in both of which qualities the Americans resemble them. It may also be due in part to the fact that the American Revolution was in a certain sense a family quarrel. A prolonged conflict of wills between the older and the younger members of the same household develops prejudices which do not easily subside. The very closeness of the family relation intensifies the misunderstanding. The seniors find it extremely difficult to comprehend the motives of the juniors, or to believe that they are really grown up. They seem like naughty and self-confident children. A person outside of the family is much more likely to see matters in their true light.

At all events, in the latter part of the eighteenth century, when Dr. Samuel Johnson was calling the Americans "a race of convicts, who ought to be thankful for anything we allow them short of hanging," and declaring that he was willing to love all mankind *except the Americans*, whom he described as "Rascals—Robbers—Pirates," a Frenchman, named Crèvecœur, who had lived some twenty years in New York, gave a different portrait of the same subject.

"What then is the American," he asks, "this new man? He is either a European or the descendant of a European, hence that strange mixture of blood which you will find in no other country. I could point out to you a family whose grandfather was an Englishman, whose wife was Dutch, whose son married a Frenchwoman, and whose present four sons have now wives of four different nations.... Here individuals of all nations are melted into a new race of men whose labours and posterity will one day cause great changes in the world. Americans are the western pilgrims, who are carrying along with them that great mass of arts, sciences, vigour, and industry which began long since in the East. They will finish the great circle."

This is the language of compliment, of course. It is the saying of a very polite prophet; and even in prophecy one is inclined to like pleasant manners. Yet that is not the reason why it seems to Americans to come much nearer to the truth than Dr. Johnson's remarks, or Charles Dickens's

American Notes, or Mrs. Trollope's *Domestic Manners of the Americans*. It is because the Frenchman has been clear-sighted enough to recognize that the Americans started out in life with an inheritance of civilized ideals, manners, aptitudes, and powers, and that these did not all come from one stock, but were assembled from several storehouses. This fact, as I have said before, is fundamental to a right understanding of American character and history. But it is particularly important to the subject of this lecture: *the sentiment of common order*, and the building-up of a settled, decent, sane life in the community.

Suppose, for example, that a family of barbarians, either from some native impulse, or under the influence of foreign visitors, should begin to civilize themselves. Their course would be slow, irregular, and often eccentric. It would alternate between servile imitation and wild originality. Sometimes it would resemble the costume of that Australian chief who arrayed himself in a stove-pipe hat and polished boots and was quite unconscious of the need of the intermediate garments.

But suppose we take an example of another kind,—let us say such a family as that which was made famous fifty years ago by a well-known work of juvenile fiction, *The Swiss Family Robinson*. They are shipwrecked on a desert island. They carry ashore with them their tastes, their habits, their ideas of what is desirable and right and fitting for decent people in the common life. It is because their souls are not naked that they do not wish their bodies to become so. It is because there is already a certain order and proportion in their minds that they organize their tasks and their time. The problem before them is not to think out a civilized existence, but to realize one which already exists within them, and to do this with the materials which they find on their island, and with the tools and implements which they save from their wrecked ship.

Here you have precisely the problem which confronted the Americans. They began housekeeping in a wild land, but not as wild people. An English lady once asked Eugene Field of Chicago whether he knew anything about his ancestors. "Not much, madam," he replied, "but I believe that mine lived in trees when they were first caught." This was an illustration of conveying truth by its opposite.

The English Pilgrims who came from Norwich and Plymouth, the Hollanders who came from Amsterdam and Rotterdam, the Huguenots who came from La Rochelle and Rouen were distinctly not tree-dwellers nor troglodytes. They were people who had the habits and preferences of a well-ordered life in cities of habitation, where the current of existence was tranquil and regular except when disturbed by the storms of war or religious persecution. And those who came from the country districts, from the little villages of Normandy and Poitou and Languedoc, of Lincolnshire and Yorkshire and Cornwall, of Friesland and Utrecht, of the Rhenish Palatinate, and of the north of Ireland, were not soldiers of fortune and adventurers. They were for the most part peaceable farmers, whose ideal of earthly felicity was the well-filled barn and the comfortable fireside.

There were people of a different sort, of course, among the settlers of America. England sent a good many of her bankrupts, incurable idlers, masterless men, sons of Belial, across the ocean in the early days. Some writers say that she sent as many as 50,000 of them. Among the immigrants of other nations there were doubtless many "who left their country for their country's good." It is silly to indulge in illusions in regard to the angelic purity and unmixed virtue of the original American stock.

But the elements of turbulence and disorder were always, and are still, in the minority. Whatever interruption they caused in the development of a civilized and decent life was local and transient. The steady sentiment of the people who were in control was in favour of common order and social coöperation.

There is a significant passage in the diary of John Adams, written just after the outbreak of mob violence against the loyalists in 1775. A man had stopped him, as he was riding along the highway, to congratulate him on the fury which the patriots and their congress had stirred up, and the general dissolution of the bonds of order.

"Oh, Mr. Adams, what great things have you and your colleagues done for us. We can never be grateful enough to you. There are no courts of justice now in this province, and I hope there will never be another." Upon which the indignant Adams comments: "Is this the object for which I have been contending, said I to myself, for I rode along without any answer to this wretch; are these the sentiments of such people, and how many of them are there in this country? Half the nation for what I know: for half the nation are debtors, if not more; and these have been in all countries the sentiments of debtors. If the power of the country should get into such hands, and there is great danger that it will, to what purpose have we sacrificed our time, our health, and everything else?"

But the fears of the sturdy old Puritan and patriot were not realized. It was not into the hands of such men as he despised and dreaded, nor even into the hands of such men as Mr. Rudyard Kipling's imaginary American,

> "Enslaved, illogical, elate ...
> Unkempt, disreputable, vast,"

that the power of the country fell. It was into the hands of men of a very different type, intelligent as well as independent, sober as well as self-reliant, inheritors of principles well-matured and defined, friends of liberty in all their policies, but at the bottom of their hearts lovers and seekers of tranquil order.

I hear the spirit of these men speaking in the words of him who was the chosen leader of the people in peace and in war. Washington retired from his unequalled public service with the sincere declaration that he wished for nothing better than to partake, "in the midst of my fellow-citizens, the benign influence of good laws under a free government, the ever favourite object of my heart, and the happy reward, as I trust, of our mutual cares, labours, and dangers."

In these nobly simple and eloquent words, the great American expresses clearly the fourth factor in the making of his country,—*the love of common order*. Here we see, in the mild light of unconscious self-revealment, one of the chief ends which the Spirit of America desires and seeks. Not merely a self-reliant life, not merely a life of equal opportunity for all, not merely an active, energetic life in which the free-will of the individual has full play, but also a life shared with one's fellow-citizens under the benign influence of good laws, a life which is controlled by principles of harmony and fruitful in efforts coöperant to a common end, a life *rangée, ordonnée, et solidaire*,—this is the American ideal.

With what difficulty men worked out this ideal in outward things in the early days we can hardly imagine. Those little communities, scattered along the edge of the wilderness, had no easy task to establish and maintain physical orderliness. Nature has her own order, no doubt, but her ways are different from man's ways; she is reluctant to submit to his control; she does not like to have her hair trimmed and her garments confined; she even communicates to man, in his first struggles with her, a little of her own carelessness, her own apparently reckless and wasteful way of doing things. "Rough and ready" is a necessary maxim of the frontier. It is hard to make a new country or a log cabin look neat.

To this day in America, even in the regions which have been long settled, one finds nothing like the excellent trimness, the precise and methodical arrangement, of the little farmsteads of the Savoy among which these lectures were written. My memory often went back, last summer, from those tiny unfenced crops laid out like the squares of a chess-board in the valleys, from those rich pastures hanging like green velvet on the steep hillsides, from those carefully tended forests of black firs, from those granges with the little sticks of wood so neatly piled along their sides under the shelter of the overhanging eaves, to the straggling fences, the fallow fields, the unkempt meadows, the denuded slopes, the shaggy underbrush, the tumbled woodpiles, and the general signs of waste and disorder which may be seen in so many farming districts of the United States. I asked myself how I could venture to assure a French audience, in spite of such apparent evidences to the contrary, that the love of order was a strong factor in the American spirit.

But then I began to remember that those farms of New England and New York and New Jersey were won only a few generations ago from a trackless and savage wilderness; that the breadth of their acres had naturally tempted the farmer to neglect the less fruitful for the more productive; that Nature herself had put a larger premium upon energy than upon parsimony in these first efforts to utilize her resources; and that, after all, what I wished to describe and prove was not an outward triumph of universal orderliness in material things, but an inward desire of order, the wish to have a common life well arranged and regulated, tranquil and steady.

Here I began to see my way more clear. Those farms of eastern America, which would look to a foreigner so rude and ill-kept, have nourished a race of men and women in whom regularity and moral steadiness and consideration of the common welfare have been characteristic traits. Their villages and towns, with few exceptions, are well cared for physically; and socially, to use a phrase which I heard from one of my guides in Maine, they are "as calm as a clock." They have their Village Improvement Societies, their Lyceum Lecture Courses, their Public Libraries, their churches (often more than they need), and their schoolhouses, usually the finest of all their buildings. They have poured into the great cities, year after year, an infusion of strong and pure American blood which has been of the highest value, not only in filling the arteries of industry and trade and the professions with a fresh current of vigorous life, but also in promoting the rapid assimilation of the mass of foreign immigrants. They have sent out a steady flood of westward-moving population which has carried with it the ideals and institutions, the customs and the habits, of common order and social coöperation.

On the crest of the advancing wave, to be sure, there is a picturesque touch of foam and fury. The first comers, the prospectors, miners, ranchers, land-grabbers, lumbermen, adventurers, are often rough and turbulent, careless of the amenities, and much given to the profanities. But they are the men who break the way and open the path. Behind them come the settlers bringing the steady life.

I could wish the intelligent foreigner to see the immense corn-fields of Indiana, Illinois, and Kansas, the vast wheat-fields of the Northwest, miles and miles of green and golden harvest, cultivated, reaped, and garnered with a skill and accuracy which resembles the movements of a mighty army. I could wish him to see the gardens and orchards of the Pacific slope, miles and miles of opulent bloom and fruitage, watered by a million streams, more fertile than the paradise of Damascus. I could wish him to see the towns and little cities which have grown up as if by magic everywhere, each one developing an industry, a social life, a civic consciousness of its own, in forms which, though often bare and simple, are almost always regular and respectable even to the point of monotony. Then perhaps he would believe that the race which has done these things in a hundred years has a real and deep instinct of common order.

But the peculiarly American quality in this instinct is its individualism. It does not wish to be organized. It wishes to organize itself. It craves form, but it dislikes formality. It prizes and cherishes the sense of voluntary effort more than the sense of obedience. It has its eye fixed on the end which it desires, a peaceable and steady life, a tranquil and prosperous community. It sometimes overlooks the means which are indirectly and obscurely serviceable to that end. It is inclined to be suspicious of any routine or convention whose direct practical benefit is not self-evident. It has a slight contempt for etiquette and manners as superficial things. Its ideal is not elegance, but utility; not a dress-parade, but a march in comradeship toward a common goal. It is reluctant to admit the value of the parade even as a discipline and preparation for the march. Often it demands so much liberty for the individual that the smooth interaction of the different parts of the community is disturbed or broken.

The fabric of common order in America is sound and strong at the centre. The pattern is well-marked, and the threads are firmly woven. But the edges are ragged and unfinished. Many of our best cities have a fringe of ugliness and filth around them which is like a torn and bedraggled petticoat on a woman otherwise well dressed.

Approaching New York, or Cincinnati, or Pittsburg, or Chicago, you pass first through a delightful region, where the homes of the prosperous are spread upon the hills, reminding you of a circle of Paradise; and then through a region of hideous disorder and new ruins, which has the aspect of a circle of Purgatory, and makes you doubt whether it is safe to go any farther for fear you may come to a worse place. This neglected belt of hideous suburbs around some of the richest cities in the world is typical and symbolical. It speaks of the haste with which things have been done; of the tendency to overlook detail, provided the main purpose is accomplished; of the lack of thoroughness, and the indifference to appearance, which are common American faults. It suggests, also, the resistance which a strong spirit of individualism offers to civic supervision and control; the tenacity with which men cling to their supposed right to keep their houses in dirt and disorder; the difficulty of making them comply with general laws of sanitation and public improvement; and the selfishness with which land-owners will leave their neglected property to disfigure the city from whose growth they expect in ten or twenty years to reap a large profit.

Yet, as a matter of fact, this very typical mark of an imperfect sense of the value of physical neatness and orderliness in American life is not growing, but diminishing. The fringes of the cities are not nearly as bad as they were thirty or forty years ago. In many of them,—notably in Philadelphia and Boston and some of the western cities,—beauty has taken the place of ugliness. Parks and playgrounds have been created where formerly there were only waste places filled with rubbish. Tumble-down shanties give way to long rows of trim little houses. Even the factories cease to look like dingy prisons and put on an air of self-respect. Nuisances are abolished. The country can draw near to the city without holding its nose.

This gradual improvement, also, is symbolical. It speaks of individualism becoming conscious of its own defects and dangers. It speaks of an effort on the part of the more intelligent and public-spirited citizens to better the conditions of life for all. It speaks of a deep instinct in the people which responds to these efforts and supports them with the necessary laws and enactments. It speaks most of all, I hope, of that underlying sense of common order which is one of the qualities of the Spirit of America.

Let me illustrate this, first, by some observations on the average American crowd.

The obvious thing about it which the foreigner is likely to notice is its good humour. It is largely made up of native optimists, who think the world is not a bad place to live in, and who have a cheerful expectation that they are going to get along in it. Although it is composed of rather excitable individuals, as a mass it is not easily thrown into passion or confusion. The emotion to which it responds most quickly is neither anger nor fear, but laughter.

But it has another trait still more striking, and that is its capacity for self-organization. Watch it in front of a ticket-office, and see how quickly and instinctively it forms "the line." No police are needed. The crowd takes care of itself. Every man finds his place, and the order once established is strictly maintained by the whole crowd. The man who tries to break it is laughed at and hustled out.

When an accident happens in the street, the throng gathers in a moment. But it is not merely curious. It is promptly helpful. There is some one to sit on the head of the fallen horse,—a dozen hands to unbuckle the harness; if a litter is needed for the wounded man, it is quickly improvised, and he is carried into the nearest shop, while some one sends a "hurry call" for the doctor and the ambulance.

Until about forty years ago, the whole work of fighting fire in the cities was left to voluntary effort. Companies of citizens were formed, like social or political clubs, which purchased fire-engines, and organized themselves into a brigade ready to come at the first alarm of a conflagration. The crowd came with them and helped. I have seen a church on Sunday morning emptied of all its able-bodied young men by the ringing of the fire-bell. It is true that there was a keen rivalry among these voluntary fire-fighters which sometimes led them to fight one another on their way to a conflagration. But out of these free associations have grown the paid fire-departments of the large cities, with their fine tradition of courage and increased efficiency.

If you wish to see an American crowd in its most extraordinary aspect, you should go to a political convention for the nomination of a President. The streets swarming with people, all hurrying in one direction, talking loudly, laughing, cheering; the vast, barn-like hall draped with red, white, and blue bunting, and packed with 12,000 of the 200,000 folks who have tried to get into it; the thousand delegates sitting together in solid cohorts according to the States which they represent, each cohort ready to shout and cheer and vote as one man for its "favourite son"; the officers on the far-away platform, Lilliputian figures facing, directing, dominating this Brobdignagian mass of humanity; the buzzing of the audience in the intervals of business; the alternate waves of excitement and uneasiness that sweep over it; the long speeches, the dull speeches, the fiery speeches, the outbreaks of laughter and applause, the coming and going of messengers, the waving of flags and banners,—what does it all mean? What reason or order is there in it? What motives guide and control this big, good-natured crowd?

Wait. You are at the Republican Convention in Chicago. The leadership of Mr. Roosevelt in the party is really the point in dispute, though not a word has been said about it. A lean, clean-cut, incisive man is speaking, the Chairman of the convention. Presently he shoots out a sentence referring to "the best abused and the most popular man in America." As if it were a signal given by a gun, that phrase lets loose a storm, a tempest of applause for Roosevelt,—cheers, yells, bursts of song, the blowing of brass-bands, the roaring of megaphones, the waving of flags; more cheers like volleys of musketry; a hurricane of vocal enthusiasm, dying down for a moment to break out in a new place, redoubling itself in vigour as if it had just begun, shaking the rafters and making the bunting flutter in the wind. For forty-seven minutes by the clock that American crowd pours out its concerted enthusiasm, and makes a new "record" for the length of a political demonstration.

Now change the scene to Denver, a couple of weeks later. The Democrats are holding their convention. You are in the same kind of a hall, only a little larger, filled with the same kind of a crowd, only more of it. The leadership of Mr. Bryan is the point in dispute, and everybody knows it. Presently a speaker on the platform mentions "the peerless son of Nebraska" and pauses as if he expected a reply. It comes like an earthquake. The crowd breaks into a long, indescribable, incredible tumult of applause, just like the other one, but lasting now for more than eighty minutes,—a new "record" of demonstration.

What are these scenes at which you have assisted? The meetings of two entirely voluntary associations of American citizens, who have agreed to work together for political purposes. And what are these masses of people who are capable of cheering in unison for three-quarters of an hour, or an hour and a quarter? Just two American crowds showing their enthusiasm for their favourites.

What does it all prove?

Nothing,—I think,—except an extraordinary capacity for self-organization.

But the Spirit of America shows the sense of common order in much deeper and more significant things than the physical smoothing and polishing of town and country, or than the behaviour of an average crowd. It is of these more important things that I wish to give some idea.

It has been said that the first instinct of the Americans, confronted by a serious difficulty or problem, is to appoint a committee and form a society. Whether this be true or not, I am sure that many, if not most, of the advances in moral and social order in the United States during the last thirty or forty years have been begun and promoted in this way. It is, in fact, the natural way in a conservative republic.

Where public opinion rules, expressing itself more or less correctly in popular suffrage, no real reform can be accomplished without first winning the opinion of the public in its favour. Those who believe in the reform must get together in order to do this. They must gather their evidence, present their arguments, show why and how certain things ought to be done, and urge the point until the public sees it.

Then, in some cases, legislation follows. The moral sense, or it may be merely the practical common sense, *le gros bon sens de ménage*, of the community, takes shape in some formal statute or enactment. A State or municipal board or commission is appointed, and the reform passes from the voluntary to the organic stage. The association or committee which promoted it disappears in a blaze of congratulation, or perhaps continues its existence to watch the enforcement of the new laws.

But there is another class of cases in which no formal legislation seems to be adequate to meet the evils, or in which the process of law-making is impeded or perhaps altogether prevented by the American system of dividing the power between the national, State, and local governments. Here the private association of public-spirited citizens must act as a compensating force in the body politic. It must take what it can get in the way of partial organic reform, and supply what is lacking by voluntary coöperation.

There is still a third class of evils which seem to have their roots not in the structure of society, but in human nature itself, and for these the typical American believes that the only amelioration is a steady and friendly effort by men of good-will. He does not look for the establishment of the millennium by statute. He does not think that the impersonal State can strengthen character, bind up broken hearts, or be a nursing mother to the ignorant, the wounded, and the helpless. For this work there must always be a personal service, a volunteer service, a service to which men and women are bound, not by authority, but by the inward ties of philanthropy and religion.

Now these three kinds of voluntary coöperation for the bettering of the common order are not peculiar to America. One finds them in every nation that has the seed of progress in its mind or the vision of the *civitas Dei* in its soul,—and nowhere more than in France. The French have a genius for society and a passion for societies. But I am not sure that they understand how much the Americans resemble them in the latter respect, and how much has been accomplished in the United States by way of voluntary social coöperation under an individualistic system.

Take the subject of hospitals. I was reading the other day a statement by M. Jules Huret:—

"At Pittsburg, the industrial hell, which contains 60,000 Italians, and 300,000 Slavs, Croats, Hungarians, etc., in the city and its suburbs,—at Pittsburg, capital of the Steel Trust, which distributes 700 millions of interest and dividends every year,—there is no free hospital!"

This is wonderfully incorrect. There are thirty-three hospitals at Pittsburgh, fifteen public and eighteen private. In 1908, thirteen of these hospitals treated over ten thousand free patients, at a cost of more than three hundred thousand dollars.

In New York there are more than forty hospitals, of which six are municipal institutions, while the others are incorporated by associations of citizens and supported largely by benevolent gifts; and more than forty free dispensaries for the treatment of patients and the distribution of medicines. In fact, the dispensaries increased so rapidly, a few years ago, that the regular physicians complained that their business was unfairly reduced. They said that prosperous people went to the dispensary to save expense; and they humbly suggested that no patient who wore diamonds should be received for free treatment.

In the United States in 1903 there were 1500 hospitals costing about $29,000,000 a year for maintenance: $9,000,000 of this came from public funds, and the remaining $20,000,000 from charitable gifts and from paying patients. One-third of the patients were in public institutions, the other two-thirds in hospitals under private or religious control. There is not a city of any consequence in America which is without good hospital accommodations; and there are few countries in the world where it is more comfortable for a stranger to break a leg or have a mild attack of appendicitis. All this goes to show that the Americans recognize the care of the sick and wounded as a part of the common order. They perceive that the State never has been, and probably never will be, able to do all that is needed without the help of benevolent individuals, religious bodies, and philanthropic societies.

How generously this help is given in America, not only for hospitals, but for all other objects of benevolence, may be seen from the fact that the public gifts and bequests of private citizens for the year 1907 amounted to more than $100,000,000.

Let me give another illustration of voluntary social coöperation in this sphere of action which lies at least in part beyond the reach of the State. In all the American cities of large size, you will find institutions which are called "Settlements,"—a vague word which has been defined to mean "homes in the poorer quarters of a city where educated men and women may live in daily contact with the working people." The first house of this kind to be established was Toynbee Hall in London, in 1885. Two years later the Neighbourhood Guild was founded in New York, and in 1889 the College Settlement in the same city, and Hull House in Chicago, were established. There are now reported some three hundred of such settlement houses in the world, of which England has 56, Holland 11, Scotland 10,

France 4, Germany 2, and the United States 207. I will take, as examples, Hull House in Chicago, and the Henry Street Settlement in New York.

Hull House was started by two ladies who went into one of the worst districts of Chicago and took a house with the idea of making it a radiating centre of orderly and happy life. Their friends backed them up with money and help. After five years the enterprise was incorporated. The buildings, which are of the most substantial kind, now cover a whole city block, some forty or fifty thousand square feet, and, include an apartment house, a boys' club, a girls' club, a theatre, a gymnasium, a day nursery, workshops, class rooms, a coffee-house, and so on. There are forty-four educated men and women in residence who are engaged in self-supporting occupations, and who give their free time to the work of the settlement. A hundred and fifty outside helpers come every week to serve as teachers, friendly visitors, or directors of clubs: 9000 people a week come to the house as members of some one of its organizations or as parts of an audience. There are free concerts, and lectures, and classes of various kinds in study and in handicraft. Investigations of the social and industrial conditions of the neighbourhood are carried on, not officially, but informally; and the knowledge thus obtained has been used not only for the visible transformation of the region around Hull House, but also to throw light upon the larger needs and possibilities of improvement in Chicago and other American cities. Hull House, in fact, is an example of ethical and humane housekeeping on a big scale in a big town.

The Henry Street Settlement in New York is quite different in its specific quality. It was begun in 1893 by two trained nurses, who went down into the tenement-house district, to find the sick and to nurse them in their homes. At first they lived in a tenement house themselves; then the growth of their work and the coming of other helpers forced them to get a little house, then another, and another, a cottage in the country, a convalescent home. The idea of the settlement was single and simple. It was to meet the need of intelligent and skilful nursing in the very places where dirt and ignorance, carelessness and superstition, were doing the most harm,—

"in the crowded warrens of the poor."

This little company of women, some twenty or thirty of them, go about from tenement to tenement, bringing cleanliness and order with them. In the presence of disease and pain they teach lessons which could be taught in no other way. They nurse five or six thousand patients every year, and make forty or fifty thousand visits. In addition to this, largely through their influence and example, the Board of Education has adopted a trained nursing service in the public schools, and has appointed a special corps of nurses to take prompt charge of cases of contagious disease among the school children. The Nurses' Settlement, in fact, is a repetition of the parable of the Good Samaritan in a crowded city instead of on a lonely road.

These two examples illustrate the kind of work that is going on all over the United States. Every religious body, Jewish or Christian, has some part in it. It touches many sides of life,—this effort to do for the common order what the State has never been able to accomplish fully,—to sweeten and humanize it. I wish that there were time to speak of some particularly interesting features, like the Children's Aid Society, the George Junior Republic, the Association for Improving the Condition of the Poor, the Kindergarten Association. But now I must pass at once to the second kind of social effort, that in which the voluntary coöperation of the citizen enlightens and guides and supplements the action of the State.

Here I might speak of the great question of the housing of the poor, and of the relation of private building and loan associations to governmental regulation of tenements and dwelling-houses. This is one of the points on which America has lagged behind the rest of the civilized world. Our excessive spirit of *laissez-faire*, and our cheerful optimism,—which in this case justifies the cynical definition of optimism as "an indifference to the sufferings of others,"—permitted the development in New York of the most congested and rottenly overcrowded ten acres on the face of the habitable globe. But the Tenement House Commission of 1894, and the other commissions which followed it, did much to improve conditions. A fairly good Tenement House Act was passed. A special Department of the municipality was created to enforce it. The dark interior rooms, the vile and unsanitary holes, the lodgings without water or air or fire-escapes, are being slowly but surely broken up and extirpated, and a half-dozen private societies, combining philanthropy with business, are building decent houses for working people, which return from 3 per cent to 5 per cent on the capital invested.

For our present purpose, however, it will be better to take an example which is less complicated, and in which the coöperation of the State and the good-will of the private citizen can be more closely and simply traced. I mean the restriction and the regulation of child labour.

Every intelligent nation sees in its children its most valuable asset. That their physical and moral development should be dwarfed or paralyzed by bondage to exhausting and unwholesome labour, or by a premature absorption in toil of any kind, would be at once a national disgrace and a national calamity.

Three kinds of societies have been and still are at work in America to prevent this shame and disaster. First, there are the societies which are devoted to the general protection of all the interests of the young, like the Society for the Prevention of Cruelty to Children.

Then there are the societies which make their appeal to the moral sense of the community to condemn and suppress all kinds of inhumanity in the conduct of industry and trade. Of these the Consumers' League is an example. Founded in New York in 1890, by a few ladies of public spirit, it has spread to twenty other States, with sixty-four distinct societies and a national organization for the whole country. Its central idea is to persuade people, rich and poor, to buy only those things which are made and sold under fair and humane conditions. The responsibility of men and women for the way in which they spend their money is recognized. They are asked to remember that the cheapness of a bargain is not the only thing for them to consider. They ought to think whether it has been made cheap at the cost of human sorrow and degradation, whether the distress and pain and exhaustion of overtasked childhood and ill-treated womanhood have made their cheap bargain a shameful and poisonous thing. The first work of the leagues was to investigate the actual condition of labour in the great stores. The law forbade them to publish a *black list* of the establishments where the employees were badly treated. That would have been in the nature of a boycott. But they ingeniously evaded this obstacle by publishing a *white list* of those which treated their people decently and kindly. Thus the standard of a *"Fair House"* where a living wage was paid, where children of tender years were not employed, where the hours of work were not excessive, and where the sanitary conditions were good, was established, and that standard has steadily been raised.

Then the leagues went on to investigate the conditions of production of the goods sold in the shops. The National League issues a *white label* which guarantees that every article upon which it is found has been manufactured in a place where, (1) the State factory law is obeyed, (2) no children under sixteen years of age are employed, (3) no night work is required and the working-day does not exceed ten hours, (4) no goods are given out to be made away from the factory. At the same time the Consumers' League has been steadily pressing the legislatures and governors of the different States for stricter and better laws in regard to the employment of women and children.

The third class of societies which are at work in this field are those which deal directly with the question of child labour. It must be remembered that under the American system this is a matter which is left to the control of the separate States. Naturally there has been the greatest imaginable diversity among them. For a long time there were many that had practically no laws upon the subject, or laws so defective that they were useless. Even now the States are far from anything like harmony or equality in their child-labour laws. Illinois, Massachusetts, New York, New Jersey, Ohio, and Wisconsin are probably in the lead in good legislation. If we may judge by the statistics of children between ten and fourteen years who are unable to read or write, Tennessee, Mississippi, the Carolinas, Louisiana, Georgia, and Alabama are in the rear.

It must be remembered, also, that the number of children between ten and fifteen years employed in manufacturing pursuits in the United States increased from 1890 to 1900 more than twice as fast as the population of the country, and that the Census of 1900 gives the total of bread-winners under fifteen years of age as 1,750,000. A graphic picture of the actual condition of child labour in the United States may be found in *The Cry of the Children*, by Mrs. John Van Vorst (New York, 1908).

Here is a little army—no, a vast army—of little soldiers, whose sad and silent files are full of menace for the republic.

The principal forces arrayed against this perilous condition of things have been the special committees of the Women's Clubs everywhere, the Child-Labour Committees in different States, and finally the National Child-Labour Committee organized in 1904. Through their efforts there has been a great advance in legislation on the subject. In 1905, twenty-two States enacted laws regulating the employment of children. In 1906 there were six States which legislated, including Georgia and Iowa, which for the first time put a law against child labour on their statute-books. In 1907 eight States amended their laws. In the same year a national investigation of the subject was ordered by Congress under direction of the Federal Commissioner of Labour.

A bill was prepared which attempted to deal with the subject indirectly through that provision of the Constitution which gives Congress the power to "regulate commerce." This bill proposed to make it unlawful to transport from one State to another the product of any factory or mine in which children under fourteen years of age were employed. It was a humane and ingenious device. But it is doubtful whether it can ever be made an effective law. The best judges think that it stretches the idea of the regulation of interstate commerce beyond reasonable limits, and that the national government has no power to control industrial production in the separate States without an amendment to the Constitution. If this be true (and I am inclined to believe it is), then the best safeguard of America against the evils of child labour must be persistent action of these private associations in each community, investigating and reporting the actual conditions, awakening and stimulating the local conscience, pushing steadily for better State laws, and, when they are enacted, still working to create a public sentiment which will enforce them.

It is one thing to love your own children and care for them. It is another thing to have a wise, tender, protecting regard for all the children of your country. We wish and hope to see better and more uniform laws against child labour in America. But, after all, nothing can take the place of the sentiment of fatherhood and motherhood in patriotism. And that comes and stays only through the voluntary effort of men and women of good-will.

The last sphere in which the sense of common order in America has been expressed and promoted by social coöperation is that of direct and definite reform accomplished by legislation, as a result, at least in part, of the work of some society or committee, formed for that specific purpose. Here a small, but neat, illustration is at hand.

For many years America practised, and indeed legally sanctioned, the habit of literary piracy. Foreign authors were distinctly refused any protection in the United States for the fruit of their intellectual labours. A foreigner might make a hat, and no one could steal it. He might cultivate a crop of potatoes, and no one could take them from him without paying for them. But let him write a book, and any one could reprint it, and sell it, and make a fortune out of it, without being compelled to give the unhappy author a penny. American authors felt the shame of this state of things,— and the disorder, too, for it demoralized the book-trade and brought a mass of stolen goods into cheap competition with those which had paid an honest royalty to their makers. A Copyright League was formed which included all the well-known writers of America. After years of hard work this league secured the passage of an international copyright law which gave the same protection to the foreigner as to the American author, providing only, under the protective tariff system, that his book must be printed and manufactured in the United States.

But the most striking and important example of this kind of work is that of the Civil Service Reform Association, which was organized in 1877. Here a few words of explanation are necessary.

In the early history of the United States the number of civil offices under the national government was comparatively small, and the appointments were generally made for ability and fitness. But as the country grew, the number of offices increased with tremendous rapidity. By 1830 the so-called 'Spoils System' which regarded them as prizes of political war, to be distributed by the successful party in each election for the reward and encouragement of its adherents, became a fixed idea in the public mind. The post-offices, the custom-houses, all departments of the civil service, were treated as rich treasuries of patronage, and used first by the Democrats and then by the Republicans, to consolidate and perpetuate partisan power.

It was not a question of financial corruption, of bribery with money. It was worse. It was a question of the disorder and impurity of the national housekeeping, of the debauchment and degradation of the daily business of the State.

Notoriously unfit persons were appointed to responsible positions. The tenure of office was brief and insecure. Every presidential election threatened to make a clean sweep of the hundreds of thousands of people who were doing the necessary routine work of the nation. Federal officeholders were practically compelled to contribute to campaign expenses, and to work and fight, like a host of mercenaries, for the success of the party which kept them in place. Confusion and inefficiency prevailed everywhere.

In 1871 the condition of affairs had become intolerable. President Grant, in his first term, recommended legislation, and appointed a national civil service commission, with George William Curtis at its head. Competitive examinations were begun, and a small appropriation was made to carry on the work. But the country was not yet educated up to the reform. Congress was secretly and stubbornly opposed to it. The appropriation was withdrawn. The work of the commission was ridiculed, and in his second term, in 1875, Grant was obliged to give it up.

Then the Civil Service Reform Association, with men like George William Curtis, Carl Schurz, Dorman B. Eaton, and James Russell Lowell as its leaders, was organized. A vigorous and systematic campaign of public agitation and education was begun. Candidates for the Presidency and other elective offices were called to declare their policy on this question.

The war of opinion was fierce. The assassination of President Garfield, in 1881, was in some measure due to the feeling of hostility aroused by his known opposition to the Spoils System. His successor, Vice-President Arthur, who was supposed to be a spoilsman, surprised everybody by his loyalty to Garfield's policy on this point. And in 1883 a bill for the reform of the Civil Service was passed and a new commission appointed. The next President was Grover Cleveland, an ardent and fearless friend of the reform, who greatly increased its practical efficiency. He fought against Congress, both in his first and in his second term, to enlarge the scope and operation of the act by bringing more offices into the classified and competitive service. In his second term, by executive order, he increased the number of classified positions from forty-three thousand to eighty-seven thousand.

Presidents Harrison and McKinley worked in the same direction. And President Roosevelt, whose first national office was that of Civil Service Commissioner from 1889 to 1895, has raised and strengthened the rules, and applied the merit system to the consular service and other important departments of governmental work.

The result is that out of three hundred and twenty-five thousand positions in the executive civil service one hundred and eighty-five thousand are now classified, and appointments are made either under competitive examination or on the merit system for proved efficiency. This is an immense forward step in the promotion of common order, and it is largely the result of the work of the Civil Service Reform Association, acting upon the formation of public opinion. I believe it would be impossible for any candidate known to favour the Spoils System to be elected to the Presidency of the United States to-day.

A moment of thought will show the bearing of this illustration upon the subject which we are now considering. Here was a big, new, democratic people, self-reliant and sovereign, prosperous to a point where self-complacency was almost inevitable, and grown quite beyond the reach of external correction and control. They had fallen into wretched habits of national housekeeping. Their domestic service was disorderly and incompetent. The party politicians, on both sides, were interested in maintaining this bad service, because they made a profit out of it. The people had been hardened to it; they seemed to be either careless and indifferent, in their large, happy-go-lucky way, or else positively attached to a system which stirred everything up every four years and created unlimited opportunities for office-seeking and salary-drawing. What power could save them from their own bad judgment?

There was no higher authority to set them right. Everything was in their own hands. The case looked hopeless. But in less than thirty years the voluntary effort of a group of clear-sighted and high-minded citizens changed everything. An appeal to the sense of common order, of decency, of propriety, in the soul of the people created a sentiment which was too strong for the selfish politicians of either party to resist. The popular will was enlightened, converted, transformed, and an orderly, just, business-like administration of the Civil Service became, if not an accomplished fact, at least a universal and acknowledged aim of national desire and effort.

It is to precisely the same source that we must look with hope for the further development of harmony, and social equilibrium, and efficient civic righteousness, in American affairs. It is by precisely the same process that America must save herself from the perils and perplexities which are inherent in her own character and in the form of government which she has evolved to fit it.

That boastful self-complacency which is the caricature of self-reliance, that contempt for the minority which is the mockery of fair play, that stubborn personal lawlessness which is the bane of the strong will and the energetic temperament, can be restrained, modified, corrected, and practically conquered, only by another inward force,—the desire of common order, the instinct of social coöperation. And there is no way of stimulating this desire, of cultivating this instinct, at least for the American republic, except the way of voluntary effort and association among the men and women of good-will.

One looks with amazement upon the vast array of "societies" of all kinds which have sprung into being in the United States during the last thirty years. They cover every subject of social thought and endeavour. Their documents and pamphlets and circulars fill the mails. Their appeals for contributions and dues tax the purse. To read all that they print would be a weariness to the flesh. To attend all their meetings and conferences would wreck the most robust listener. To speak at all of them would ruin the most fluent orator. A feeling of humorous discouragement and dismay often comes over the quiet man who contemplates this astonishing phase of American activity.

But if he happens also to be a conscientious man, he is bound to remember, on the other side, that the majority of these societies exist for some practical end which belongs to the common order. The Women's Clubs, all over the country, have been powerful promoters of local decency and good legislation. The Leagues for Social Service, for Political Education, for Municipal Reform, have investigated conditions, collected facts, and acted as "clearing-houses for human betterment." The White Ribbon, and Red Ribbon, and Blue Ribbon Clubs have worked for purity and temperance. The Prison Associations have sought to secure the treatment of criminals as human beings. The City Clubs, and Municipal Leagues, and Vigilance Societies have acted as unpaid watchmen over the vital interests of the great cities. The Medical and Legal Societies have used their influence in behalf of sanitary reform and the improvement of the machinery and methods of the courts.

There is no subject affecting the common welfare on which Congress would venture to legislate to-day until the committee to which the bill had been referred had first given a public hearing. At these hearings, which are open to all, the societies that are interested present their facts and arguments, and plead their cause.

Even associations of a less serious character seem to recognize their civic responsibilities. The Society of the Sons of the Revolution prints and distributes, in a dozen different languages, a moral and patriotic pamphlet of "Information for Immigrants." The Sportsmen's Clubs take an active interest in the improvement and enforcement of laws for the protection of fish and game. The Audubon Societies in many parts of the country have stopped, or at least checked, the extermination of wild birds of beauty and song for the supposed adornment of women's hats.

It cannot be denied that there are still many and grave defects in the common order of America. For example, when a bitter and prolonged conflict between organized capital and organized labour paralyzes some necessary industry, we have no definite and sure way of protecting that great third party, the helpless consuming public. In the coal strike, a few years ago, the operators and the workmen were at a deadlock, and there was a good prospect that many people would freeze to death. But President Roosevelt, with the approval of men like ex-President Cleveland, forced or persuaded the two warring parties to go on with the mining of coal, while a committee of impartial arbitration settled their dispute.

We have no uniformity in our game laws, our forestry laws, our laws for the preservation and purity of the local water-supply. As these things are left to the control of the separate States, it will be very difficult to bring them all into harmony and good order.

The same thing is true of a much more important matter,—the laws of marriage and divorce. Each State and Territory has its own legislation on this subject. In consequence there are fifty-one distinct divorce codes in the United States and their Territories. South Carolina grants no divorce; New York and North Carolina admit only one cause; New Hampshire admits fourteen. In some of the States, like South Dakota, a legal residence of six months is sufficient to qualify a person to sue for a divorce; and those States have always a transient colony of people who are anxious to secure a rapid separation.

The provisions in regard to re-marriage are various and confusing. A man who is divorced under the law of South Dakota and marries again can be convicted of bigamy in New York.

All this is immensely disorderly and demoralizing. The latest statistics which are accessible show that there were 25,000 divorces in the United States in the year 1886. The annual number at present is estimated at nearly 60,000.

But the work which is being done by the National League for the Protection of the Family, and the united efforts of the churches, which have been deeply impressed with the need of awakening and elevating public sentiment on this subject, have already produced an improvement in many States. It is possible that a much greater uniformity of legislation may be reached, even though a national law may not be feasible. It is certain that the effective protection of the family must be secured in America, as elsewhere, by a social education and coöperation which will teach men and women to think of the whole subject "reverently, soberly, and in the fear of God, duly considering the causes for which marriage was ordained."

In this, and in all other things of like nature, we Americans look into the future not without misgivings and fears, but with an underlying confidence that the years will bring a larger and nobler common order, and that the Republic will be peace.

In the minor problems we shall make many mistakes. In the great problems, in the pressing emergencies, we rely upon the moral power in reserve. The sober soul of the people is neither frivolous nor fanatical. It is earnest, ethical, desirous of the common good, responsive to moral appeal, capable of self-control, and, in the time of need, strong for self-sacrifice. It has its hours of illusion, its intervals of indifference and drowsiness. But while there are men and women passionately devoted to its highest ideals, and faithful in calling it to its duties, it will not wholly slumber nor be lost in death.

If there is to be an American aristocracy, it shall not be composed of the rich, nor of those whose only pride is in their ancient name, but of those who have done most to keep the Spirit of America awake and eager to solve the problems of the common order, of those who have spoken to her most clearly and steadily, by word and deed, reminding her that

> "By the Soul
> Only, the Nations shall be great and free."

VI
PERSONAL DEVELOPMENT AND EDUCATION

The Spirit of America shows its ingrained individualism nowhere more clearly than in education. First, by the breadth of the provision which it makes, up to a certain point, for everybody who wishes to be educated. Second, by the entire absence of anything like a centralized control of education. Third, by the remarkable evolution of different types of educational institutions and the liberty of choice which they offer to each student.

All this is in the nature of evidence to the existence of a fifth quality in the Spirit of America, closely connected with the sense of self-reliance and a strong will-power, intimately related to the love of fair play and common order,—a keen appreciation of *the value of personal development*.

Here again, as in the previous lectures, what we have to observe and follow is not a logical syllogism, nor a geometrical proposition neatly and accurately worked out. It is a natural process of self-realization. It is the history of the soul of a people learning how to think for itself. As in government, in social order, in organized industry, so in education, America has followed, not the line of least resistance, nor the line of abstract doctrine, but the line of vital impulse.

And whence did this particular impulse spring? From a sense of the real value of knowledge to man as man. From a conviction that there is no natural right more precious than the right of the mind to grow. From a deep instinct of prudence reminding a nation in which the people are the sovereign that it must attend to "the education of the prince."

These are the feelings and convictions, very plain and primitive in their nature, which were shared by the real makers of America, and which have ever since controlled her real leaders. They are in striking contrast with the views expressed by some of the strangers who were sent out in early times to govern the colonies; as, for example, that Royal Governor Berkeley who, writing home to England from Virginia in the seventeenth century, thanked God that "no public schools nor printing-presses existed in the colony," and added his "hope that they would not be introduced for a hundred years, since learning brings irreligion and disobedience into the world, and the printing-press disseminates them and fights against the best intentions of the government."

But this Governor Berkeley was of a different type from that Bishop Berkeley who came to the western world to establish a missionary training-school, and, failing in that, gave his real estate at Newport and his library of a thousand books to the infant Yale College at New Haven; of a different type from those Dutch colonists of New Amsterdam who founded the first American public school in 1621; of a different type from those Puritan colonists of Massachusetts Bay who established the Boston Latin School in 1635 and Harvard College in 1636; of a different type from Franklin, who founded the Philadelphia Circulating Library in 1731, the American Philosophical Society in 1744, and the Academy of Pennsylvania in 1749; of a different type from Washington, who urged the foundation of a national university and left property for its endowment by his last will and testament; of a different type from Jefferson, who desired to have it recorded upon his tombstone that he had rendered three services to his country—the framing of the Declaration of Independence, the establishment of religious liberty in Virginia, and the founding of the University of that State.

Among the men who were most responsible, from the beginning, for the rise and growth and continuance of the spirit of self-reliance and fair play, of active energy and common order in America, there was hardly one who did not frequently express his conviction that the spread of public intelligence was necessary to these ends. Among those who have been most influential in the guidance of the republic, nothing is more remarkable than their agreement in the opinion that education, popular and special, is friendly to republican institutions.

This agreement is not a mere formal adherence to an academic principle learned in the same school. For there has been the greatest possible difference in the schooling of these men. Adams, Jefferson, Madison, Monroe, Hamilton, Webster, Hayes, Garfield, Harrison, Roosevelt, had a college training; Washington, Franklin, Marshall, Jackson, Van Buren, Clay, Lincoln, Cleveland, McKinley, did not.

The sincere respect for education which is typical of the American spirit is not a result of education. It is a matter of intuitive belief, of mental character, of moral temperament. First of all, the sure conviction that every American child ought to have the chance to go to school, to learn to read, to write, to think; second, the general notion that it is both fair and wise to make an open way for every one who is talented and ambitious to climb as far as he can and will in the higher education; third, the vague feeling that it will be to the credit and benefit of democracy not only to raise the average level of intelligence, but also to produce men and institutions of commanding excellence in learning and science and philosophy,—these are the three elements which you will find present in varying degrees in the views of typical Americans in regard to education.

I say that you will find these elements in varying degrees, because there has been, and there still is, some divergence of opinion as to the comparative emphasis to be laid on these three points—the schoolhouse door open to everybody, the college career open to all the talents, and the university providing unlimited opportunities for the disinterested pursuit of knowledge.

Which is the most important? How far may the State go in promoting the higher education? Is it right to use the public funds, contributed by all the taxpayers, for the special advantage of those who have superior intellectual powers? Where is the line to be drawn between the education which fits a boy for citizenship, and that which merely gratifies his own tastes or promotes his own ambition?

These are questions which have been seriously, and, at times, bitterly debated in America. But, meantime, education has gone steadily and rapidly forward. The little public school of New Amsterdam has developed into an enormous common-school system covering the United States and all their Territories. The little Harvard College at Cambridge has become the mother of a vast brood of institutions, public and private, which give all kinds of instruction, philosophical, scientific, literary, and technical, and which call themselves colleges or universities according to their own fancy and will.

A foreigner visiting the country for the first time might well think it had a touch of academic mania. A lecturer invited to describe the schools and colleges of the United States in a single discourse might well feel as embarrassed as that famous diplomat to whom his companion at dinner said, between the soup and the fish, "I am so glad to meet you, for now you can tell me all about the Far Eastern Question and make me understand it." Let me warn you against expecting anything of that kind in this lecture. I am at least well enough educated to know that it is impossible to tell all about American education in an hour. The most that I can hope to do is to touch on three points:—

First, the absence of centralized control and the process of practical unification in educational work in the United States.

Second, the growth and general character of the common schools as an expression of the Spirit of America.

Third, the relation of the colleges, universities, and technical institutes to the life of the republic.

I. First, it should be distinctly understood and remembered that there is absolutely *no national system of education in America.*

The government at Washington has neither power nor responsibility in regard to it. There is no Ministry of Public Instruction; there are no Federal Inspectors; there is no regulation from the centre. The whole thing is local and voluntary to a degree which must seem to a Frenchman incomprehensible if not reprehensible. In consequence it is both simple and complicated,—simple in its practical working, and extremely complicated in its general aspect.

The reasons for this lack of a national system and a centralized control are not far to seek. In the first place, at the time when the Union was formed, many different European influences were already at work fostering different educational ideals in various parts of the country. No doubt the English influence was predominant, especially in New England. Harvard College at Cambridge in Massachusetts may be regarded as the legitimate child of Emmanuel College at Cambridge in England. But the development of free common schools, especially in the Middle States, was more largely affected by the example of Holland, France, and Switzerland than by England. The Presbyterians of New Jersey, when they founded Princeton College in 1746, naturally turned to Scotland for a model.

In Virginia, through Thomas Jefferson, a strong French influence was felt. A Frenchman, Quesnay, who had fought in the American army of the Revolution, proposed to establish a National Academy of Arts and Sciences in Richmond, with branches at Baltimore, Philadelphia, and New York, to give advanced instruction in all branches of human learning. He had the approval of many of the best people in France and Virginia, and succeeded in raising 60,000 francs towards the endowment. The corner-stone of a building was laid, and one professor was chosen. But the scheme failed, because, in 1786, both America and France were busy and poor. Jefferson's plan for the University of Virginia, which was framed on French lines, was put into successful operation in 1825.

It would have been impossible at any time in the early history of the United States—indeed, I think it would be impossible now—to get a general agreement among the friends of education in regard to the form and method of a national system.

Another obstacle to a national system was the fact that the colleges founded before the Revolution—William and Mary, Harvard, Yale, Princeton, Columbia—were practically supported and controlled by different churches—Congregational, Presbyterian, or Episcopalian. Churches are not easy to combine.

Still another obstacle, and a more important one, was the sentiment of local independence, the spirit of home rule which played such a prominent part in the *mise en scène* of the American drama. Each of the distinct States composing the Union was tenacious of its own individuality, and jealous of the local rights by which alone that individuality could be preserved. The most significant and potent of these rights was that of educating the children and youth of the community.

The States which entered the Union later brought with them the same feeling of local pride and responsibility. Ohio with its New England traditions, Kentucky with its Southern traditions, Michigan with its large infusion of French blood and thought, Wisconsin with its vigorous German and Scandinavian element,—each of these communities felt competent and in honour bound to attend to its own educational affairs. So far as the establishment and control of schools, colleges, and universities is concerned, every State of the Union is legally as independent of all the other States as if they were separate European countries like France and Germany and Switzerland. Therefore, we may say that the American system of education is not to have a system.

But if we stop here, we rest upon one of those half-truths which are so dear to the pessimist and the satirist. The bare statement that there is no national system of education in America by no means exhausts the subject. Taken by itself, it gives a false impression. Abstract theory and formal regulation are not the only means of unification. Nature and human nature have their own secrets for creating unity in diversity. This is the process which has been at work in American education.

First of all, there has been a general agreement among the States in regard to the vital necessity of education in a republic. The constitution of Massachusetts, adopted in 1780, reads thus: "Wisdom and knowledge, as well as virtue, diffused generally among the people, being necessary for the preservation of their rights and liberties; and as these depend on spreading the opportunities and advantages of education in the various parts of the country, and among the different orders of the people, it shall be the duty of legislatures and magistrates, in all future periods of this Commonwealth, to cherish the interests of literature and the sciences, and all seminaries of them, especially the university at Cambridge, public schools, and grammar schools in the towns; to encourage private societies and public institutions, rewards and immunities, for the promotion of agriculture, arts, sciences, commerce, trades, manufactures, and a natural history of the country; to countenance and inculcate the principles of humanity and general benevolence, public and private charity, industry and frugality, honesty and punctuality, in their dealings, sincerity, good humour, and all social affections and generous sentiments among the people." After such a sentence, one needs to take breath. It is a full programme of American idealism, written in the English of the eighteenth century, when people had plenty of time. The new constitution of North Carolina adopted in 1868 puts the same idea in terse modern style: "The people have the right to the privilege of education, and it is the duty of the State to guard and maintain that right." You will find the same principle expressed in the constitutions of all the American commonwealths.

In the next place, the friendly competition and rivalry among the States produced a tendency to unity in education. No State wished to be left behind. The Southern States, which for a long time had neglected the matter of free common schools, were forced by the growth of illiteracy, after the Civil War, to provide for the schooling of all their children at public expense. The Western States, coming into the Union one by one, had a feeling of pride in offering to their citizens facilities for education which should be at least equal to those offered in "the effete East." It is worthy of note that the most flourishing State Universities now are west of the Alleghanies. The only States which have more than 90 per cent of the children from five to eighteen years of age enrolled in the common schools are Colorado, Nevada, Idaho, and Washington,—all in the far West.

Furthermore, the free intercourse and exchange of population between the States have made for unity in the higher education. Methods which have proved successful in one community have been imitated and adopted in others. Experiments tried at Harvard, Yale, Princeton, or Columbia have been repeated in the West and South. Teachers trained in the older colleges have helped to organize and develop the new ones.

Nor has this process of assimilation been confined to American ideas and models. European methods have been carefully studied and adapted to the needs and conditions of the United States. I happen to know of a new Institute of Technology which has been recently founded in Texas by a gift of eight millions of dollars. The president-elect is a scientific man who has already studied in France and Germany and achieved distinction in his department. But before he touches the building and organization of his new Institute, he is sent to Europe for a year to see the oldest and the newest and the best that has been done there. In fact, the Republic of Learning to-day is the true Cosmopolis. It knows no barriers of nationality. It seeks truth and wisdom everywhere, and wherever it finds them, it claims them for its own.

The spirit of voluntary coöperation for the promotion of the common order, of which I spoke in a previous lecture, has made itself felt in education by the formation of Teachers' Associations in the various States, and groups of States, and by the foundation of the National Educational

Association, a voluntary body incorporated in the District of Columbia, "to elevate the character and advance the interests of the profession of teaching, and to promote the cause of education in the United States."

Finally, while there is no national centre of authority for education in the United States, there is a strong central force of encouragement and enlightenment. The Federal Government shows its interest in education in several ways: First, in the enormous grants of public lands which it has made from the beginning for the endowment of common schools and higher institutions in the various States.

Second, in the control and support of the United States Military Academy at West Point, the Naval Academy at Annapolis, the Indian Schools, the National Museum, and the Congressional Library, and in the provision which it makes for agricultural and mechanical schools in different parts of the country. The annual budget for these purposes runs from twelve to twenty millions of dollars a year.

Third, in the establishment of a National Bureau of Education which collects statistics and information and distributes reports on all subjects connected with the educational interests of America. The Commissioner at the head of this bureau is a man of high standing and scholarship. He is chosen without reference to politics, and holds his office independent of party. He has no authority to make appointments or regulations. But he has a large influence, through the light which he throws upon the actual condition of education, in promoting the gradual and inevitable process of unification.

Let me try to sum up what I have been saying on this difficult subject of the lack of system and the growth of unity in American education. There is no organization from the centre. But there is a distinct organization from the periphery,—if I may use a scientific metaphor of such an unscientific character. The formative principle is the development of the individual.

What, then, does the average American boy find in this country to give him a series of successive opportunities to secure this personal development of mental and moral powers?

First, a public primary school and grammar school which will give him the rudiments of learning from his sixth to his fourteenth year. Then a public high school which will give him about what a French *lycée* gives from his fourteenth to his eighteenth year. He is now ready to enter the higher education. Up to this point, if he lives in a town of any considerable size, he has not been obliged to go away from home. Many of the smaller places of three or four thousand inhabitants have good high schools. If he lives in the country, he may have had to go to the nearest city or large town for his high school or academy.

Beyond this point, he finds either a college, as it is called in America, or the collegiate department in one of the universities, which will give him a four years' course of general study. Before he can begin this, he must pass what is called an entrance examination, which is practically uniform in all the better institutions, and almost, but perhaps not quite, equivalent to the examination in France for the degree of *bachelier*. Thus a certain standard of preparation is set for all the secondary schools. It is at the end of his general course in literature, science, and philosophy that the American student gets his bachelor's degree, which corresponds pretty nearly to the French degree of *licencié* in letters and sciences.

Now the student, a young man of about twenty-one or twenty-two years, is supposed to be prepared, either to go into the world as a fairly well-educated citizen, or to continue his studies for a professional career. He finds the graduate schools of the universities ready to give him courses which lead to the degree of M.A. or Ph.D., and prepare him for the higher kind of teaching. The schools of law and medicine and engineering offer courses of from two to four years with a degree of LL.B. or M.D. or C.E. or M.E. at the end of them. The theological seminaries are ready to instruct him for the service of the church in a course of three or four years.

By this time he is twenty-four or twenty-five years old. Unless he has special ambitions which lead him to study abroad, or to take up original research at Johns Hopkins, Harvard, Columbia, Cornell, or some other specially equipped university, he is now ready for practical work. The American theory is that he should go to work and get the rest of his education in practice.

Of course there have been short cuts and irregular paths open to him all along the way,—a short cut from the high school to the technical school,—a short cut into law or medicine by the way of private preparation for the examination, which in some States is absurdly low. But these short cuts are being closed up very rapidly. It is growing more and more difficult to get into a first-class professional school without a collegiate or university degree. Already, if the American student wants system and regularity, he can get a closely articulated course, fitted to his individual needs, from the primary school up to the door of his profession.

But the real value of that course depends upon two things that are beyond the power of any system to insure—the personal energy that he brings to his work, and the personal power of the professors under whom he studies. I suppose the same thing is true in France as in America.

Neither here nor there can you find equality of results. All you have a right to expect is equality of opportunity.

II. The great symbol and instrument of this idea of equal opportunity in the United States is the common school. In every State of the Union provision is made for the education of the children at public expense. The extent and quality of this education, the methods of control, the standards of equipment, even the matter of compulsory or voluntary attendance, vary in different States and communities. But, as a rule, you may say that it puts within the reach of every boy and girl free instruction from the *a-b-c* up to the final grade of a *lycée*.

The money expended by the States on these common schools in 1905-1906 was $307,765,000,—more than one-third of the annual expenditure of the national government for all purposes, more than twice as much as the State governments spent for all other purposes. This sum, you understand, was raised by direct, local taxation. Neither the import duties nor the internal revenue contributed anything to it. It came directly from the citizen's pocket, at the rate of $3.66 a year *per capita*, or nearly $13 a year for every grown-up man.

How many children were benefited by it? Who can tell? 16,600,000 boys and girls were enrolled in the public schools (that is to say, more than 70 per cent of the whole number of children between five and eighteen years of age, and about 20 per cent of the total population). The teachers employed were 109,000 men, 356,000 women. The average daily expenditure for each pupil was 17 cents; the average annual expenditure, about $25.

In addition to this number there are at least 1,500,000 children in privately endowed and supported schools, secular or religious. The Catholic Church has a system of parochial schools which is said to provide for about a million children. Many of the larger Protestant Churches support high schools and academies of excellent quality. Some of the most famous secondary schools, like Phillips Exeter and Andover, St. Paul's, the Hill School, Lawrenceville School, are private foundations well endowed.

These figures do not mean much to the imagination. Statistics are like grapes in their skins. You have to put a pressure upon them to extract any wine. Observe, then, that if you walked through an American town between eight and nine in the morning, and passed a thousand people indoors and out, more than two hundred of them would be children going to school. Perhaps twenty of these children would turn in at private schools, or church schools. But nine-tenths of the little crowd would be on their way to the public schools. The great majority of the children would be under fourteen years of age; for only about one child out of every twenty goes beyond that point in schooling. Among the younger children the boys would outnumber the girls a little. But in the small group of high-school children there would be three girls to two boys, because the boys have to go to work earlier to earn a living.

Suppose you followed one of these groups of children into the school, what would you find? That would depend entirely upon local circumstances. You might find a splendid building with modern fittings; you might find an old-fashioned building, overcrowded and ill-fitted. Each State, as I have said before, has its own common-school system. And not only so, but within the State there are smaller units of organization—the county, the township, the school district. Each of these may have its own school board, conservative or progressive, generous or stingy, and the quality and equipment of the schools will vary accordingly. They represent pretty accurately the general enlightenment and moral tone of the community.

Wealth has something to do with it, of course. People cannot spend money unless they have it. The public treasury is not a Fortunatus' purse which fills itself. In the remote country districts, the little red schoolhouse, with its single room, its wooden benches, its iron stove, its unpainted flagstaff, stands on some hill-top without a tree to shadow it, in brave, unblushing poverty. In the richer cities there are common school palaces with an aspect of splendour which is almost disconcerting.

Yet it is not altogether a question of wealth. It is also a question of public spirit. Baltimore is nearly as large and half as rich as Boston, yet Boston spends about three times as much on her schools. Richmond has about the same amount of taxable property as Rochester, N.Y., yet Richmond spends only one-quarter as much on her schools. Houston, Texas; Wilmington, Delaware; Harrisburg, Pennsylvania; Trenton, New Jersey; New Bedford, Massachusetts; and Des Moines, Iowa, are six cities with a population of from 80,000 to 100,000 each, and not far apart in wealth. But their public-school bills in 1906 varied as follows: Des Moines, $492,000; New Bedford, $472,000; Harrisburg, $304,000; Trenton, $300,000; Wilmington, $226,000; and Houston, the richest of the six, $163,000.

If you should judge from this that the public schools are most liberally supported in the North Atlantic, North Central, and Far Western States, you would be right. The amount that is contributed to the common schools per adult male inhabitant is largest in the following States in order: Utah, $22; North Dakota, $21; New York, $20; Colorado, $20; Massachusetts, $19; South Dakota, $19; Nebraska, $17; and Pennsylvania, $16. The comparative weakness of the common schools in the South Atlantic and

South Central States has led to the giving of large sums of money by private benevolence, the Peabody Fund, the Slater Fund, the Southern Education Fund, which are administered by boards of trustees for the promotion of education in these backward regions. The Spirit of America strongly desires to spread, to improve, to equalize and coördinate, the public schools of the whole country.

Is it succeeding? What lines is it following? Where are the changes most apparent?

First of all, there is a marked advance in the physical equipment of the common school. In the villages and in the rural districts the new buildings are larger and more commodious than the old ones. In many parts of the country the method of concentration is employed. Instead of half a dozen poor little schoolhouses scattered over the hills, one good house is built in a central location, and the children are gathered from the farmhouses by school omnibuses or by the electric trolley-cars. Massachusetts made a law in 1894 requiring every township which did not have a high school to pay the transportation expenses of all qualified pupils who wished to attend the high schools of neighbouring towns.

In many States text-books are provided at the public cost. In the cities the increased attention to the physical side of things is even more noticeable. No expense is spared to make the new buildings attractive and convenient. Libraries and laboratories, gymnasiums and toilet-rooms, are provided. In some cities a free lunch is given to the pupils.

The school furniture is of the latest and most approved pattern. The old idea of the adjustable child who could be fitted to any kind of a seat or desk, has given way to the new idea of the adjustable seat and desk which can be fitted to any kind of a child. School doctors are employed to make a physical examination of the children. In a few cities there are school nurses to attend to the pupils who are slightly ailing.

Physical culture, in the form of calisthenics, military drill, gymnastics, is introduced. Athletic organizations, foot-ball clubs, base-ball clubs, are encouraged among the boys. In every way the effort is apparent to make school life attractive, more comfortable, more healthful.

Some critics say that the effort is excessive, that it spoils and softens the children, that it has distracted their attention from the serious business of hard study. I do not know. It is difficult for a man to remember just how serious he was when he was a boy. Perhaps the modern common-school pupil is less Spartan and resolute than his father used to be. Perhaps not. Pictures on the wall and flowers in the window, gymnastics and music, may not really distract the attention more than uncomfortable seats and bad ventilation.

Another marked tendency in the American common school, at least in the large towns and cities, is the warm, one might almost say feverish, interest in new courses and methods of study. In the primary schools this shows itself chiefly in the introduction of new ways of learning to spell and to cipher. The alphabet and the multiplication table are no longer regarded as necessities. The phonetic pupil is almost in danger of supposing that reading, writing, and arithmetic are literally "the three *r*'s." Hours are given to nature-study, object-lessons, hygiene. Children of tender years are instructed in the mysteries of the digestive system. The range of mental effort is immensely diversified.

In the high schools the increase of educational novelties is even more apparent. The courses are multiplied and divided. Elective studies are offered in large quantity. I take an example from the programme of a Western high school. The studies required of all pupils are: English, history, algebra, plane geometry, biology, physics, and Shakespeare. The studies offered for a choice are: psychology, ethics, commercial law, civics, economics, arithmetic, book-keeping, higher algebra, solid geometry, trigonometry, penmanship, phonography, drawing and the history of art, chemistry, Latin, German, French, Spanish, and Greek. This is quite a rich intellectual bill of fare for boys and girls between fourteen and eighteen years old. It seems almost encyclopædic,—though I miss a few subjects like Sanskrit, Egyptology, photography, and comparative religions.

The fact is that in the American high schools, as in the French *lycées* the effort to enlarge and vary the curriculum by introducing studies which are said to be "urgently required by modern conditions" has led to considerable confusion of educational ideals. But with us, while the extremes are worse, owing to the lack of the central control, the disorder is less universal, because the conservative schools have been free to adhere to a simpler programme. It is a good thing, no doubt, that the rigidity of the old system, which made every pupil go through the same course of classics and mathematics, has been relaxed. But our danger now lies in the direction of using our schools to fit boys and girls to make a living, rather than to train them in a sound and vigorous intellectual life. For this latter purpose it is not true that all branches of study are of equal value. Some are immensely superior. We want not the widest range, but the best selection.

There are some points in which the public schools of America, so far as one can judge from the general reports, are inferior to those of France. One of these points, naturally, is in the smooth working that comes from uniformity and coördination. Another point, strangely enough, is in the careful provision for moral instruction in the primary schools. At least in the programmes of the French schools, much more time and attention are given to this than in the American programmes.

Another point of inferiority in the United States is in the requirement of proper preparation and certification of all teachers; and still another is in the security of their tenure of office and the length of their service in the profession. The teaching force of the American schools is a noble army; but it would be more efficient if the regular element were larger in proportion to the volunteers. The *personnel* changes too often.

One reason for this, no doubt, is the fact that the women outnumber the men by three to one. Not that the women are poorer teachers. Often, especially in primary work, they are the best. But their average term of professional service is not over four years. They are interrupted by that great accident, matrimony, which invites a woman to stop teaching, and a man to continue.

The shortage of male teachers, which exists in so many countries, is felt in extreme form in the United States. Efforts are made to remedy it by the increase of normal schools and teachers' colleges, and by a closer connection between the universities and the public-school system.

In the conduct and development of the common schools we see the same voluntary, experimental, pragmatic way of doing things that is so characteristic of the Spirit of America in every department of life. "Education," say the Americans, "is desirable, profitable, and necessary. The best way for us to get it is to work it out for ourselves. It must be practically adapted to the local conditions of each community, and to the personal needs of the individual. The being of the child must be the centre of development. What we want to do is to make good citizens for American purposes. Liberty must be the foundation, unity the superstructure."

This, upon the whole, is what the common schools are doing for the United States: Three-fourths of the children of the country (boys and girls studying together from their sixth to their eighteenth year) are in them. They are immensely democratic. They are stronger in awakening the mind than in training it. They do more to stimulate quick perception than to cultivate sound judgment and correct taste. Their principles are always good, their manners sometimes. Universal knowledge is their foible; activity is their temperament; energy and sincerity are their virtues; superficiality is their defect.

Candour compels me to add one more touch to this thumb-nail sketch of the American common school. The children of the rich, the socially prominent, the higher classes, if you choose to call them so, are not generally found in the public schools. At least in the East and the South, most of these children are educated in private schools and academies.

One cause of this is mere fashion. But there are two other causes which may possibly deserve to be called reasons, good or bad.

The first is the fear that coeducation, instead of making the boys refined and the girls hardy, as it is claimed, may effeminate the boys and roughen the girls.

The second is the wish to secure more thorough and personal teaching in smaller classes. This the private schools offer, usually at a high price. In the older universities and colleges, a considerable part, if not the larger number, of the student body, comes from private preparatory schools and academies. Yet it must be noted that of the men who take high honours in scholarship a steadily increasing number, already a majority, are graduates of the free public high schools.

This proves what? That the State can give the best if it wants to. That it is much more likely to want to do so if it is enlightened, stimulated, and guided by the voluntary effort of the more intelligent part of the community.

III. This brings me to the last division of the large subject around which I have been hastily circling: the institutions of higher education,—universities, colleges, and technological schools. Remember that in America these different names are used with bewildering freedom. They are not definitions, nor even descriptions; they are simply "tags." A school of arts and trades, a school of modern languages, may call itself a university. An institution of liberal studies, with professional departments and graduate schools attached to it, may call itself a college. The size and splendour of the label does not determine the value of the wine in the bottle. The significance of an academic degree in America depends not on the name, but on the quality, of the institution that confers it.

But, generally speaking, you may understand that a college is an institution which gives a four years' course in liberal arts and sciences, for which four years of academic preparation are required: a university adds to this, graduate courses, and one or more professional schools of law, medicine, engineering, divinity, or pedagogy; a technological school is one in which the higher branches of the applied arts and sciences are the chief subjects of study and in which only scientific degrees are conferred.

Of these three kinds of institutions, 622 reported to the United States Bureau of Education in 1906: 158 were for men only; 129 were for women only; 335 were coeducational. The number of professors and instructors was 24,000. The number of undergraduate and resident graduate students was 136,000. The income of these institutions for the year was $40,000,000, of which a little less than half came from tuition fees, and a little more than half from gifts and endowments. The value of the real estate and equipment was about $280,000,000, and the invested funds for endowment amounted to $236,000,000.

These are large figures. But they do not convey any very definite idea to the mind, until we begin to investigate them and ask what they mean. How did this enormous enterprise of higher education come into being? Who supports it? What is it doing?

There are three ways in which the colleges and universities of America have originated. They have been founded by the churches to "provide a learned and godly ministry, and to promote knowledge and sound intelligence in the community." They have been endowed by private and personal gifts and benefactions. They have been established by States, and in a few cases by cities, to complete and crown the common-school system.

But note that in the course of time important changes have occurred. Most of the older and larger universities which were at first practically supported and controlled by churches, have now become independent and are maintained by non-sectarian support. The institutions which remain under control of churches are the smaller colleges, the majority of which were established between 1810 and 1870.

The universities established by a large gift or bequest from a single person, of which Johns Hopkins in Maryland, Leland Stanford in California, and Chicago University founded by the head of the Standard Oil Company, may be taken as examples, are of comparatively recent origin. Their immediate command of large wealth has enabled them to do immense things quickly. Chicago is called by a recent writer "a University by enchantment."

In the foundation of State universities the South pointed the way with the Universities of Tennessee North Carolina, and Georgia, at the end of the eighteenth century. But since that time the West has distinctly taken the lead. Out of the twenty-nine colleges and universities which report an enrolment of over a thousand undergraduate and graduate students, sixteen are State institutions, and fourteen of these are west of the Alleghanies.

It is in these State universities, especially in the Middle West, in Michigan, Wisconsin, Illinois, Minnesota, Iowa, that you will see the most remarkable illustration of that thirst for knowledge, that ambition for personal development, which is characteristic of the Spirit of Young America.

The thousands of sons and daughters of farmers, mechanics, and tradesmen, who flock to these institutions, are full of eagerness and hope. They are no respecters of persons, but they have a tremendous faith in the power of education. They all expect to succeed in getting it, and to succeed in life by means of it. They are alert, inquisitive, energetic; in their work strenuous, and in their play enthusiastic. They diffuse around them an atmosphere of joyous endeavour,—a nervous, electric, rude, and bracing air. They seem irreverent; but for the most part they are only intensely earnest and direct. They pursue their private aim with intensity. They "want to know." They may not be quite sure what it is that they want to know. But they have no doubt that knowledge is an excellent thing, and they have come to the university to get it. This strong desire to learn, this attitude of concentrated attack upon the secrets of the universe, seems to me less noticeable among the students of the older colleges of the East than it is in these new big institutions of the Centre.

The State universities which have developed it, or grown up to meet it, are in many cases wonderfully well organized and equipped. Professors of high standing have been brought from the Eastern colleges and from Europe. The main stress, perhaps, is laid upon practical results, and the technique of industry. Studies which are supposed to be directly utilitarian take the precedence over those which are regarded as merely disciplinary. But in the best of these institutions the idea of general culture is maintained.

The University of Michigan, which is the oldest and the largest of these western State universities, still keeps its primacy with 4280 students drawn from 48 States and Territories. But the Universities of Wisconsin, and Minnesota, and Illinois, and California are not unworthy rivals.

A member of the British Commission which came to study education in the United States four years ago gave his judgment that the University of Wisconsin was the foremost in America. Why? "Because," said he, "it is a wholesome product of a commonwealth of three millions of people; sane, industrial, and progressive. It knits together the professions and labours; it makes the fine arts and the anvil one."

That is a characteristic modern opinion, coming, mark you, not from an American, but from an Englishman. It reminds me of the advice which an old judge gave to a young friend who had just been raised to the judicial bench. "Never give reasons," said he, "for your decisions. The decision may often be right, but the reasons will probably be wrong."

A thoughtful critic would say that the union of "the fine arts and the anvil" was not a sufficient ground for awarding the primacy to a university. Its standing must be measured in its own sphere,—the realm of knowledge and wisdom. It exists for the disinterested pursuit of truth, for the development of the intellectual life, and for the rounded development of character. Its primary aim is not to fit men for any specific industry, but to give them those things which are everywhere essential to intelligent living. Its attention must be fixed not on the work, but on the man. In him, as a person, it must seek to develop four powers—the power to see clearly, the power to imagine vividly, the power to think independently, and the power to will wisely and nobly. This is the university ideal which a conservative critic would maintain against the utilitarian theory. He might admire the University of Wisconsin greatly, but it would be for other reasons than those which the Englishman gave.

"After all," this conservative would say, "the older American universities are still the most important factors in the higher education of the country. They have the traditions. They set the standard. You cannot understand education in England without going to Oxford and Cambridge, nor in America without going to Harvard, Yale, Princeton, and Columbia."

Perhaps the conservative would be right. At all events, I wish that I could help the friendly foreign observer to understand just what these older institutions of learning, and some others like them, have meant and still mean to Americans. They are the monuments of the devotion of our fathers to ideal aims. They are the landmarks of the intellectual life of the young republic. Time has changed them, but it has not removed them. They still define a region within which the making of a reasonable man is the main interest, and truth is sought and served for her own sake.

Originally, these older universities were almost identical in form. They were called colleges and based upon the idea of a uniform four years' course consisting mainly of Latin, Greek, and mathematics, with an addition of history, philosophy, and natural science in the last two years, and leading to the degree of Bachelor of Arts. This was supposed to be the way to make a reasonable man.

But in the course of time the desire to seek truth in other regions, by other paths, led to a gradual enlargement and finally to an immense expansion of the curriculum. The department of letters was opened to receive English and other modern languages. The department of philosophy branched out into economics and civics and experimental psychology. History took notice of the fact that much has happened since the fall of the Roman Empire. Science threw wide its doors to receive the new methods and discoveries of the nineteenth century. The elective system of study came in like a flood from Germany. The old-fashioned curriculum was submerged and dissolved. The four senior colleges came out as universities and began to differentiate themselves.

Harvard, under the bold leadership of President Eliot, went first and farthest in the development of the elective system. One of its own graduates, Mr. John Corbin, has recently written of it as "a Germanized university." It offers to its students free choice among a multitude of courses so great that it is said that one man could hardly take them all in two hundred years. There is only one course which every undergraduate is required to take,—English composition in the Freshman year: 551 distinct courses are presented by the Faculty of Arts and Sciences. In the whole university there are 556 officers of instruction and 4000 students. There is no other institution in America which provides such a rich, varied, and free chance for the individual to develop his intellectual life.

Princeton, so far as the elective system is concerned, represents the other extreme. President McCosh introduced it with Scotch caution and reserve, in 1875. It hardly went beyond the liberalizing of the last two years of study. Other enlargements followed. But at heart Princeton remained conservative. It liked regularity, uniformity, system, more than it liked freedom and variety. In recent years it has rearranged the electives in groups, which compel a certain amount of unity in the main direction of a student's effort. It has introduced a system of preceptors or tutors who take personal charge of each student in his reading and extra class-room work. The picked men of the classes, who have won prizes, or scholarships, or fellowships, go on with higher university work in the graduate school. The divinity school is academically independent, though closely allied. There are no other professional schools. Thus Princeton is distinctly "a collegiate university," with a very definite idea of what a liberal education ought to include, and a fixed purpose of developing the individual by leading him through a regulated intellectual discipline.

Yale, the second in age of the American universities, occupies a middle ground, and fills it with immense vigour. Very slow in yielding to the elective system, Yale theoretically adopted it four years ago in its extreme form. But in practice the "Yale Spirit" preserves the unity of each class from entrance to graduation; the "average man" is much more of a controlling factor than he is at Harvard, and the solid body of students in the Department of Arts and Sciences gives tone to the whole university. Yale is typically American in its love of liberty and its faculty of self-organization. It draws its support from a wider range of country than either Harvard or Princeton. It has not been a leader in the production of advanced ideas or educational methods. Originality is not its mark. Efficiency is. No other American university has done more in giving men of light and leading to industrial, professional, and public life in the United States.

Columbia, by its location in the largest of the American cities, and by the direction which its last three presidents have given to its policy, has become much stronger in its professional schools and its advanced graduate work, than in its undergraduate college. Its schools of mines and law and medicine are famous. In its graduate courses it has as many students enrolled as Harvard, Yale, and Michigan put together. It has a library of 450,000 volumes, and endowment for various kinds of special study, including Chinese and journalism.

None of these four universities is coeducational in the department of arts and sciences. But Harvard and Columbia each have an annex for women,—Radcliffe College and Barnard College,—in which the university professors lecture and teach.

In Yale, Harvard, Princeton, and most of the older colleges, except those which are situated in the great cities, there is a common life of the students which is peculiar, I believe, to America, and highly characteristic and interesting. They reside together in large halls or dormitories grouped in an academic estate which is almost always beautiful with ancient trees and spacious lawns. There is nothing like the caste division among them which is permitted, if not fostered, at Oxford and Cambridge by the existence of distinct colleges in the same university. They belong to the same social body, a community of youth bound together for a happy interval of four years between the strict discipline of school and the separating pressure of life in the outer world. They have their own customs and traditions, often absurd, always picturesque and amusing. They have their own interests, chief among which is the cultivation of warm friendships among men of the same age. They organize their own clubs and societies, athletic, musical, literary, dramatic, or purely social, according to elective affinity. But the class spirit creates a ground of unity for all who enter and graduate together, and the college spirit makes a common tie for all.

It is a little world by itself,—this American college life,—incredibly free, yet on the whole self-controlled and morally sound,—physically active and joyful, yet at bottom full of serious purpose. See the students on the athletic field at some great foot-ball or base-ball match; hear their volleying cheers, their ringing songs of encouragement or victory; watch their waving colours, their eager faces, their movements of excitement as the fortune of the game shifts and changes; and you might think that these young men cared for nothing but out-of-door sport. But that noisy enthusiasm is the natural overflow of youthful spirits. The athletic game gives it the easiest outlet, the simplest opportunity to express college loyalty by an outward sign, a shout, a cheer, a song. Follow the same men from day to day, from week to week, and you will find that the majority of them, even among the athletes, know that the central object of their college life is to get an education. But they will tell you, also, that this education does not come only from the lecture-room, the class, the library. An indispensable and vital part of it comes from their daily contact with one another in play and work and comradeship,—from the chance which college gives them to know, and estimate, and choose, their friends among their fellows.

It is intensely democratic,—this American college life,—and therefore it has distinctions, as every real democracy must. But they are not artificial and conventional. They are based in the main upon what a man is and does, what contribution he makes to the honour and joy and fellowship of the community.

The entrance of the son of a millionnaire, of a high official, of a famous man, is noted, of course. But it is noted only as a curious fact of natural history which has no bearing upon the college world. The real question is, What kind of a fellow is the new man? Is he a good companion; has he the power of leadership; can he do anything particularly well; is he a vigorous and friendly person? Wealth and parental fame do not count, except perhaps as slight hindrances, because of the subconscious jealousy which they arouse in a community where the majority do not possess them. Poverty does not count at all, unless it makes the man himself proud and shy, or confines him so closely to the work of self-support that he has no time to mix with the crowd. Men who are working their own way through college are often the leaders in popularity and influence.

I do not say that there are no social distinctions in American college life. There, as in the great world, little groups of men are drawn together by expensive tastes and amusements; little coteries are formed which aim at exclusiveness. But these are of no real account in the student body. It lives in a brisk and wholesome air of free competition in study and sport, of free intercourse on a human basis.

It is this tone of humanity, of sincerity, of joyful contact with reality, in student life, that makes the American graduate love his college with a sentiment which must seem to foreigners almost like sentimentality. His memory holds her as the *Alma Mater* of his happiest years. He goes back to visit her halls, her playgrounds, her shady walks, year after year, as one returns to a shrine of the heart. He sings the college songs, he joins in the college cheers, with an enthusiasm which does not die as his voice loses the ring of youth. And when gray hairs come upon him, he still walks with his class among the old graduates at the head of the commencement procession. It is all a little strange, a little absurd, perhaps, to one who watches it critically, from the outside. But to the man himself it is simply a natural tribute to the good and wholesome memory of American college life.

But what are its results from the educational point of view? What do these colleges and universities do for the intellectual life of the country? Doubtless they are still far from perfect in method and achievement. Doubtless they let many students pass through them without acquiring mental thoroughness, philosophical balance, fine culture. Doubtless they need to advance in the standard of teaching, the strictness of examination, the encouragement of research. They have much to learn. They are learning.

Great central institutions like those which Mr. Carnegie has endowed for the Promotion of Research and for the Advancement of Teaching will help progress. Conservative experiments and liberal experiments will lead to better knowledge.

But whatever changes are made, whatever improvements arrive in the higher education in America, one thing I hope will never be given up,—the free, democratic, united student life of our colleges and universities. For without this factor we cannot develop the kind of intellectual person who will be at home in the republic. The world in which he has to live will not ask him what degrees he has taken. It will ask him simply what he is, and what he can do. If he is to be a leader in a country where the people are sovereign, he must add to the power to see clearly, to imagine vividly, to think independently, and to will wisely, the faculty of knowing other men as they are, and of working with them for what they ought to be. And one of the best places to get this faculty is in the student life of an American college.

VII
SELF-EXPRESSION AND LITERATURE

All human activity is, in a certain sense, a mode of self-expression. The works of man in the organization of the State, in the development of industry, in voluntary effort for the improvement of the common order, are an utterance of his inner life.

But it is natural for him to seek a fuller, clearer, more conscious mode of self-expression, to speak more directly of his ideals, thoughts, and feelings. It is this direct utterance of the Spirit of America, as it is found in literature, which I propose now, and in the following lectures,[1] to discuss.

Around the political and ecclesiastical and social structures which men build for themselves there are always flowing great tides and currents of human speech; like the discussions in the studio of the architect, the confused murmur of talk among the workmen, the curious and wondering comments of the passing crowd, when some vast cathedral or palace or hall of industry is rising from the silent earth. Man is a talking animal. The daily debates of the forum and the market-place, the orations and lectures of a thousand platforms, the sermons and exhortations of the thousand pulpits, the ceaseless conversation of the street and the fireside, all confess that one of the deepest of human appetites and passions is for self-expression and intercourse, to reveal and to communicate the hidden motions of the spirit that is in man.

Language, said a cynic, is chiefly useful to conceal thought. But that is only a late-discovered, minor, and decadent use of speech. If concealment had been the first and chief need that man felt, he never would have made a language. He would have remained silent. He would have lived among the trees, contented with that inarticulate chatter which still keeps the thoughts of monkeys (if they have any) so well concealed.

But vastly the greater part of human effort toward self-expression serves only the need of the transient individual, the passing hour. It sounds incessantly beneath the silent stars,—this murmur, this roar, this *susurrus* of mingled voices,—and melts continually into the vague inane. The idle talk of the multitude, the eloquence of golden tongues, the shouts of brazen throats, go by and are forgotten, like the wind that passes through the rustling leaves of the forest.

In the fine arts man has invented not only a more perfect and sensitive, but also a more enduring, form for the expression of that which fills his spirit with the joy and wonder of living. His sense of beauty and order; the response of something within him to certain aspects of nature, certain events of life; his interpretation of the vague and mysterious things about him which seem to suggest a secret meaning; his delight in the intensity and clearness of single impressions, in the symmetry and proportion of related objects; his double desire to surpass nature, on the one side by the simplicity and unity of his work, or on the other side by the freedom of its range and the richness of its imagery; his sudden glimpses of truth; his persistent visions of virtue; his perception of human misery and his hopes of human excellence; his deep thoughts and solemn dreams of the Divine,—all these he strives to embody, clearly or vaguely, by symbol, or allusion, or imitation, in painting and sculpture, music and architecture.

The medium of these arts is physical; they speak to the eye and the ear. But their ultimate appeal is spiritual, and the pleasure which they give goes far deeper than the outward senses.

In literature we have another art whose very medium is more than half spiritual. For words are not like lines, or colours, or sounds. They are living creatures begotten in the soul of man. They come to us saturated with human meaning and association. They are vitally related to the emotions and thoughts out of which they have sprung. They have a wider range, a more delicate precision, a more direct and penetrating power than any other medium of expression.

The art of literature which weaves these living threads into its fabric lies closer to the common life and rises higher into the ideal life than any other art. In the lyric, the drama, the epic, the romance, the fable, the *conte*, the essay, the history, the biography, it not only speaks to the present hour, but also leaves its record for the future.

Literature consists of those writings which interpret the meanings of nature and life, in words of charm and power, touched with the personality of the author, in artistic forms of permanent interest.

Out of the common utterances of men, the daily flood of language spoken and written, by which they express their thoughts and feelings,— out of that current of journalism and oratory, preaching and debate, literature comes. But with that current it does not pass away. Art has endowed it with the magic which confers a distinct life, a longer endurance, a so-called immortality. It is the ark on the flood. It is the light on the candlestick. It is the flower among the leaves, the consummation of the plant's vitality, the crown of its beauty, the treasure-house of its seeds.

Races and nations have existed without a literature. But their life has been dumb. With their death their power has departed.

What does the world know of the thoughts and feelings of those unlettered tribes of white and black and yellow and red, flitting in ghost-like pantomime across the background of the stage? Whatever message they may have had for us, of warning, of encouragement, of hope, of guidance, remains undelivered. They are but phantoms, mysterious and ineffective.

But with literature life arrives at utterance and lasting power. The Scythians, the Etruscans, the Phœnicians, the Carthaginians, have vanished into thin air. We grope among their ruined cities. We collect their figured pottery, their rusted coins and weapons. And we wonder what manner of men they were. But the Greeks, the Hebrews, the Romans, still live. We know their thoughts and feelings, their loves and hates, their motives and ideals. They touch us and move us to-day through a vital literature. Nor should we fully understand their other arts, nor grasp the meaning of their political and social institutions without the light which is kindled within them by the ever-burning torch of letters.

The Americans do not belong among the dumb races. Their spiritual descent is not from Etruria and Phœnicia and Carthage, nor from the silent red man of the western forests. Intellectually, like all the leading races of Europe, they inherit from Greece and Rome and Palestine.

Their instinct of self-expression in the arts has been slower to assert itself than those other traits which we have been considering,—self-reliance, fair-play, common order, the desire of personal development. But they have taken part, and they still take part (not altogether inaudibly), in the general conversation and current debate of the world. Moreover, they have begun to create a native literature which utters, to some extent at least, the thoughts and feelings of the soul of the people.

This literature, considered in its *ensemble* as an expression of our country, raises some interesting questions which I should like to answer. Why has it been so slow to begin? Why is it not more recognizably American? What are the qualities in which it really expresses the Spirit of America?

I. If you ask me why a native literature has been so slow to begin in America, I answer, first, *that it has not been slow at all*. Compared with other races, the Americans have been rather less slow than the average in seeking self-expression in literary form and in producing books which have survived the generation which produced them.

How long was it, for example, before the Hebrews began to create a literature? A definite answer to that question would bring us into trouble with the theologians. But at least we may say that from the beginning of the

Hebrew Commonwealth to the time of the prophet Samuel there were three centuries and a half without literature.

How long did Rome exist before its literary activities began? Of course we do not know what books may have perished. But the first Romans whose names have kept a place in literature were Nævius and Ennius, who began to write more than five hundred years after the city was founded.

Compared with these long periods of silence, the two hundred years between the settlement of America and the appearance of Washington Irving and James Fenimore Cooper seems but a short time.

Even earlier than these writers I should be inclined to claim a place in literature for two Americans,—Jonathan Edwards and Benjamin Franklin. Indeed it is possible that the clean-cut philosophical essays of the iron-clad Edwards, and the intensely human autobiography of the shrewd and genial Franklin may continue to find critical admirers and real readers long after many writers, at present more praised, have been forgotten.

But if you will allow me this preliminary protest against the superficial notion that the Americans have been remarkably backward in producing a national literature, I will make a concession to current and commonplace criticism by admitting that they were not as quick in turning to literary self-expression as might have been expected. They were not a mentally sluggish people. They were a race of idealists. They were fairly well educated. Why did they not go to work at once, with their intense energy, to produce a national literature on demand?

One reason, perhaps, was that they had the good sense to perceive that a national literature never has been, and never can be, produced in this way. It is not made to order. It grows.

Another reason, no doubt, was the fact that they already had more books than they had time to read. They were the inheritors of the literature of Europe. They had the classics and the old masters. Milton and Dryden and Locke wrote for them. Pope and Johnson, Defoe and Goldsmith, wrote for them. Cervantes and Le Sage wrote for them. Montesquieu and Rousseau wrote for them. Richardson and Smollett and Fielding gave them a plenty of long-measure novels. Above all, they found an overflowing supply of books of edification in the religious writings of Thomas Fuller, Richard Baxter, John Bunyan, Philip Doddridge, Matthew Henry, and other copious Puritans. There was no pressing need of mental food for the Americans. The supply was equal to the demand.

Another reason, possibly, was the fact that they did not have a new language, with all its words fresh and vivid from their origin in life, to develop and exploit. This was at once an advantage and a disadvantage.

English was not the mother-tongue of all the colonists. For two or three generations there was a confusion of speech in the middle settlements. It is recorded of a certain young Dutchwoman from New Amsterdam, travelling to the English province of Connecticut, that she was in danger of being tried for witchcraft because she spoke a diabolical tongue, evidently marking her as "a child of Satan."

But this polyglot period passed away, and the people in general spoke

"the tongue that Shakespeare spoke,"—

spoke it indeed rather more literally than the English did, retaining old locutions like "I guess," and sprinkling their talk with "Sirs," and "Ma'ams,"—which have since come to be considered as Americanisms, whereas they are really Elizabethanisms.

The possession of a language that is already consolidated, organized, enriched with a vast vocabulary, and dignified by literary use, has two effects. It makes the joyful and unconscious literature of adolescence, the period of popular ballads and rhymed chronicles, quaint animal-epics and miracle-plays, impossible. It offers to the literature of maturity an instrument of expression equal to its needs.

But such a language carries with it discouragements as well as invitations. It sets a high standard of excellence. It demands courage and strength to use it in any but an imitative way.

Do not misunderstand me here. The Americans, since that blending of experience which made them one people, have never felt that the English language was strange or foreign to them. They did not adopt or borrow it. It was their own native tongue. They grew up in it. They contributed to it. It belonged to them. But perhaps they hesitated a little to use it freely and fearlessly and originally while they were still in a position of tutelage and dependence. Perhaps they waited for the consciousness that they were indeed grown up,—a consciousness which did not fully come until after the War of 1812. Perhaps they needed to feel the richness of their own experience, the vigour of their own inward life, before they could enter upon the literary use of that most rich and vigorous of modern languages.

Another reason why American literature did not develop sooner was the absorption of the energy of the people in other tasks than writing. They had to chop down trees, to build houses, to plough prairies. It is one thing to explore the wilderness, as Chateaubriand did, an elegant visitor looking for the materials of romance. It is another thing to live in the wilderness and fight with it for a living. Real pioneers are sometimes poets at heart. But they seldom write their poetry.

After the Americans had won their security and their daily bread in the wild country, they had still to make a State, to develop a social order, to provide themselves with schools and churches, to do all kinds of things which demand time, and toil, and the sweat of the brow. It was a busy world. There was more work to be done than there were workmen to do it. Industry claimed every talent almost as soon as it got into breeches.

A Franklin, who might have written essays or philosophical treatises in the manner of Diderot, must run a printing-press, invent stoves, pave streets, conduct a postal service, raise money for the War of Independence. A Freneau, who might have written lyrics in the manner of André Chénier, must become a soldier, a sea-captain, an editor, a farmer.

Even those talents which were drawn to the intellectual side of life were absorbed in the efforts which belong to the current discussions of affairs, the daily debate of the world, rather than to literature. They disputed, they argued, they exhorted, with a direct aim at practical results in morals and conduct. They became preachers, orators, politicians, pamphleteers. They wrote a good deal; but their writing has the effect of reported speech addressed to an audience. The mass of sermons, and political papers, and long letters on timely topics, which America produced in her first two hundred years is considerable. It contains much more vitality than the imitative essays, poems, and romances of the same period.

John Dickinson's "Letters from a Pennsylvania Farmer," the sermons of President Witherspoon of Princeton, the papers of Madison, Hamilton, and Jay in the *Federalist*, are not bad reading, even to-day. They are virile and significant. They show that the Americans knew how to use the English language in its eighteenth-century form. But they were produced to serve a practical purpose. Therefore they lack the final touch of that art whose primary aim is the pleasure of self-expression in forms as permanent and as perfect as may be found.

II. The second question which I shall try to answer is this: Why is not the literature of America, not only in the beginning but also in its later development, more distinctly American?

The answer is simple: *It is distinctly American.* But unfortunately the critics who are calling so persistently and looking so eagerly for "Americanism" in literature, do not recognize it when they see it.

They are looking for something strange, eccentric, radical, and rude. When a real American like Franklin, or Irving, or Emerson, or Longfellow, or Lanier, or Howells appears, these critics will not believe that he is the genuine article. They expect something in the style of "Buffalo Bill." They imagine the Spirit of America always in a red shirt, striped trousers, and rawhide boots.

They recognize the Americanism of Washington when he crosses the forest to Fort Duquesne in his leather blouse and leggings. But when he appears at Mount Vernon in black velvet and lace ruffles, they say, "This is no American after all, but a transplanted English squire." They acknowledge that Francis Parkman is an American when he follows the Oregon trail on horseback in hunter's dress. But when he sits in the tranquil library of his West Roxbury home surrounded by its rose gardens, they say, "This is no American, but a gentleman of Europe in exile."

How often must our critics be reminded that the makers of America were not redskins nor amiable ruffians, but rather decent folk, with perhaps an extravagant admiration for order and respectability? When will they learn that the descendants of these people, when they come to write books, cannot be expected to show the qualities of barbarians and iconoclasts? How shall we persuade them to look at American literature not for the by-product of eccentricity, but for the self-expression of a sane and civilized people? I doubt whether it will ever be possible to effect this conversion and enlightenment; for nothing is so strictly closed against criticism as the average critic's adherence to the point of view imposed by his own limitations. But it is a pity, in this case, that the point of view is not within sight of the facts.

There is a story that the English poet Tennyson once said that he was glad that he had never met Longfellow, because he would not have liked to see the American poet put his feet upon the table. If the story is true, it is most laughable. For nothing could be more unlike the super-refined Longfellow than to put his feet in the wrong place, either on the table, or in his verse. Yet he was an American of the Americans, the literary idol of his country.

It seems to me that the literature of America would be more recognizable if those who consider it from the outside knew more of the real spirit of the country. If they were not always looking for volcanoes and earthquakes, they might learn to identify the actual features of the landscape.

But when I have said this, honesty compels me to go a little further and admit that the full, complete life of America still lacks an adequate expression in literature. Perhaps it is too large and variegated in its outward forms, too simple in its individual types, and too complex in their combination, ever to find this perfect expression. Certainly we are still waiting for "the great American Novel."

It may be that we shall have to wait a long time for this comprehensive and significant book which will compress into a single cup of fiction all the different qualities of the Spirit of America, all the fermenting elements that mingle in the vintage of the New World. But in this hope deferred,—if indeed it be a hope that can be reasonably entertained at all,—we are in no worse estate than the other complex modern nations. What English novel gives a perfect picture of all England in the nineteenth century? Which of the French romances of the last twenty years expresses the whole spirit of France?

Meantime it is not difficult to find certain partial and local reflections of the inner and outer life of the real America in the literature, limited in amount though it be, which has already been produced in that country. In some of it the local quality of thought or language is so predominant as to act almost as a barrier to exportation. But there is a smaller quantity which may fairly be called "good anywhere"; and to us it is, and ought to be, doubly good because of its Americanism.

Thus, for example, any reader who understands the tone and character of life in the Middle States, around New York and Philadelphia, in the first quarter of the nineteenth century, feels that the ideas and feelings of the more intelligent people, those who were capable of using or of appreciating literary forms, are well enough represented in the writings of the so-called "Knickerbocker School."

Washington Irving, the genial humorist, the delicate and sympathetic essayist and story-teller of *The Sketch-Book*, was the first veritable "man of letters" in America. Cooper, the inexhaustible teller-of-tales in the open air, the lover of brave adventure in the forest and on the sea, the Homer of the backwoodsman, and the idealist of the noble savage, was the discoverer of real romance in the New World.

Including other writers of slighter and less spontaneous talent, like Halleck, Drake, and Paulding, this school was marked by a cheerful and optimistic view of life, a tone of feeling more sentimental than impassioned, a friendly interest in humanity rather than an intense moral enthusiasm, and a flowing, easy style,—the manner of a company of people living in comfort and good order, people of social habits, good digestion, and settled opinions, who sought in literature more of entertainment and relaxation than of inspiration or what the strenuous reformers call "uplift."

After the days when its fashionable idol was Willis, and its honoured though slightly cold poet was Bryant, and its neglected and embittered genius was Edgar Allan Poe, this school, lacking the elements of inward coherence, passed into a period of decline. It revived again in such writers as George William Curtis, Donald Mitchell, Bayard Taylor, Charles Dudley

Warner, Frank R. Stockton; and it continues some of its qualities in the present-day writers whose centre is undoubtedly New York.

Is it imaginary, or can I really feel some traces, here and there, of the same influences which affected the "Knickerbocker School" in such different writers as Mark Twain and William Dean Howells, in spite of their western origin? Certainly it can be felt in essayists like Hamilton Mabie and Edward S. Martin and Brander Matthews, in novelists like Dr. Weir Mitchell and Hopkinson Smith, in poets like Aldrich and Stedman, and even in the later work of a native lyrist like Richard Watson Gilder. There is something,—I know not what,—a kind of *urbanum genus dicendi*, which speaks of the great city in the background and of a tradition continued. Even in the work of such a cosmopolitan and relentless novelist as Mrs. Wharton, or of such an independent and searching critic as Mr. Brownell, my mental palate catches a flavour of America and a reminiscence of New York; though now indeed there is little or nothing left of the Knickerbocker optimism and cheerful sentimentality.

The American school of historians, including such writers as Ticknor, Prescott, Bancroft, Motley, and Parkman, represents the growing interest of the people of the New World for the history of the Old, as well as their desire to know more about their own origin and development. Motley's *Rise of the Dutch Republic*, Parkman's volumes on the French settlements in Canada, Sloane's *Life of Napoleon*, and Henry C. Lea's *History of the Inquisition* are not only distinguished works of scholarship, but also eminently readable and interesting expressions of the mind of a great republic considering important events and institutions in other countries to which its own history was closely related. The serious and laborious efforts of Bancroft to produce a clear and complete *History of the United States* resulted in a work of great dignity and value. But much was left for others to do in the way of exploring the sources of the nation, and in closer study of its critical epochs. This task has been well continued by such historians as John Fiske, Henry Adams, James Bach McMaster, John Codman Ropes, James Ford Rhodes, Justin Winsor, and Sydney G. Fisher.

These are only some of the principal names which may be cited to show that few countries have better reason than the United States to be proud of a school of historians whose works are not only well documented, but also well written, and so entitled to be counted as literature.

The Southern States, before the Civil War and for a little time after, were not largely represented in American letters. In prose they had a fluent romancer, Simms, who wrote somewhat in the manner of Cooper, but with less skill and force; an exquisite artist of the short-story and the lyric, Poe, who, although he was born in Boston and did most of his work in

Philadelphia and New York, may perhaps be counted sympathetically with the South; two agreeable story-tellers, John Esten Cooke and John P. Kennedy; two delicate and charming lyrists, Paul Hayne and Henry Timrod; and one greatly gifted poet, Sidney Lanier, whose career was cut short by a premature death.

But the distinctive spirit of the South did not really find an adequate utterance in early American literature, and it is only of late years that it is beginning to do so. The fine and memorable stories of George W. Cable reflect the poesy and romance of the creole life in Louisiana. James Lane Allen and Thomas Nelson Page express in their prose the Southern atmosphere and temperament. The poems of Madison Cawein are full of the bloom and fragrance of Kentucky. Among the women who write, Alice Hegan Rice, "Charles Egbert Craddock," Ruth McEnery Stuart, "George Madden Martin," and Mary Johnston may be named as charming story-tellers of the South. Joel Chandler Harris has made the old negro folk-tales classic, in his *Uncle Remus*,—a work which belongs, if I mistake not, to one of the most enduring types of literature.

But beyond a doubt the richest and finest flowering of *belles lettres* in the United States during the nineteenth century was that which has been called "the Renaissance of New England." The quickening of moral and intellectual life which followed the Unitarian movement in theology, the antislavery agitation in society, and the transcendental fermentation in philosophy may not have caused, but it certainly influenced, the development of a group of writers, just before the middle of the century, who brought a deeper and fuller note into American poetry and prose.

Hawthorne, profound and lonely genius, dramatist of the inner life, master of the symbolic story, endowed with the double gift of deep insight and exquisite art; Emerson, herald of self-reliance and poet of the intuitions, whose prose and verse flash with gem-like thoughts and fancies, and whose calm, vigorous accents were potent to awaken and sustain the intellectual independence of America; Longfellow, the sweetest and the richest voice of American song, the household poet of the New World; Whittier, the Quaker bard, whose ballads and lyrics reflect so perfectly the scenery and the sentiment of New England; Holmes, genial and pungent wit, native humorist, with a deep spring of sympathy and a clear vein of poetry in his many-sided personality; Lowell, generous poet of high and noble emotions, inimitable writer of dialect verse, penetrating critic and essayist,—these six authors form a group not yet equalled in the literary history of America.

The factors of strength, and the hidden elements of beauty, in the Puritan character came to flower and fruit in these men. They were liberated, enlarged, quickened by the strange flood of poetry, philosophy, and romantic sentiment which flowed into the somewhat narrow and sombre enceinte of Yankee thought and life. They found around them a circle of eager and admiring readers who had felt the same influences. The circle grew wider and wider as the charm and power of these writers made itself felt, and as their ideas were diffused. Their work, always keeping a distinct New England colour, had in it a substance of thought and feeling, an excellence of form and texture, which gave it a much broader appeal. Their fame passed from the sectional to the national stage. In their day Boston was the literary centre of the United States. And in after days, though the sceptre has passed, the influence of these men may be traced in almost all American writers, of the East, the West, or the South, in every field of literature, except perhaps the region of realistic or romantic fiction.

Here it seems as if the West had taken the lead. Bret Harte, with his frontier stories, always vivid but not always accurate, was the founder of a new school, or at least the discoverer of a new mine of material, in which Frank Norris followed with some powerful work, too soon cut short by death, and where a number of living men like Owen Wister, Stewart Edward White, and O. Henry are finding graphic stories to tell. Hamlin Garland, Booth Tarkington, William Allen White, and Robert Herrick are vigorous romancers of the Middle West. Winston Churchill studies politics and people in various regions, while Robert Chambers explores the social complications of New York; and both write novels which are full of interest for Americans and count their readers by the hundred thousand.

In the short-story Miss Jewett, Miss Wilkins, and Mrs. Deland have developed characteristic and charming forms of a difficult art. In poetry George E. Woodberry and William Vaughn Moody have continued the tradition of Emerson and Lowell in lofty and pregnant verse. Joaquin Miller has sung the songs of the Sierras, and Edwin Markham the chant of labour. James Whitcomb Riley has put the very heart of the Middle West into his familiar poems, humorous and pathetic.

And Walt Whitman, the "democratic bard," the poet who broke all the poetic traditions? Is it too soon to determine whether his revolution in literature was a success, whether he was a great initiator or only a great exception? Perhaps so. But it is not too soon to recognize the beauty of feeling and form, and the strong Americanism, of his poems on the death of Lincoln, and the power of some of his descriptive lines, whether they are verse or rhapsodic prose.

It is evident that such a list of names as I have been trying to give must necessarily be very imperfect. Many names of substantial value are omitted. The field is not completely covered. But at least it may serve to indicate some of the different schools and sources, and to give some idea of the large literary activity in which various elements and aspects of the Spirit of America have found and are finding expression.

III. The real value of literature is to be sought in its power to express and to impress. What relation does it bear to the interpretation of nature and life in a certain country at a certain time? That is the question in its historical form. How clearly, how beautifully, how perfectly, does it give that interpretation in concrete works of art? That is the question in its purely æsthetic form. What personal qualities, what traits of human temperament and disposition does it reveal most characteristically in the spirit of the land? That is the question in the form which belongs to the study of human nature.

It is in this last form that I wish to put the question, just now, in order to follow logically the line marked by the general title of these lectures. The Spirit of America is to be understood not only by the five elements of character which I have tried to sketch in outline,—the instinct of self-reliance, the love of fair-play, the energetic will, the desire of order, the ambition of self-development. It has also certain temperamental traits; less easy to define, perhaps; certainly less clearly shown in national and social institutions, but not less important to an intimate acquaintance with the people.

These temperamental traits are the very things which are most distinctive in literature. They give it colour and flavour. They are the things which touch it with personality. In American literature, if you look at it broadly, I think you will find four of these traits most clearly revealed,—a strong religious feeling, a sincere love of nature, a vivid sense of humour, and a deep sentiment of humanity.

(1) It may seem strange to say that a country which does not even name the Supreme Being in its national constitution, which has no established form of worship or belief, and whose public schools and universities are expressly disconnected from any kind of church control, is at the same time strongly religious, in its temperament. Yet strange as this seems, it is true of America.

The entire independence of Church and State was the result of a deliberate conviction, in which the interest of religion was probably the chief consideration. In the life of the people the Church has been not less, but more, potent than in most other countries. Professor Wendell was perfectly right in the lectures which he delivered in Paris four years ago, when he laid so much emphasis upon the influence of religion in determining the course of thought and the character of literature in America. Professor Münsterberg is thoroughly correct when he says in his excellent book *The Americans*, "The entire American people are in fact profoundly religious, and have been, from the day when the Pilgrim Fathers landed, down to the present moment."

The proof of this is not to be seen merely in outward observance, though I suppose there is hardly any other country, except Scotland, in which there is so much church-going, Sabbath-keeping, and Bible-reading. It is estimated that less than fifteen of the eighty millions of total population are entirely out of touch with any church. But all this might be rather superficial, formal, conventional. It might be only a hypocritical cover for practical infidelity. And sometimes when one reads the "yellow journals" with their flaming exposures of social immorality, industrial dishonesty, and political corruption, one is tempted to think that it may be so.

Yet a broader, deeper, saner view,—a steady look into the real life of the typical American home, the normal American community,—reveals the fact that the black spots are on the surface and not in the heart of the country.

The heart of the people at large is still old-fashioned in its adherence to the idea that every man is responsible to a higher moral and spiritual power,—that duty is more than pleasure,—that life cannot be translated in terms of the five senses, and that the attempt to do so lowers and degrades the man who makes it,—that religion alone can give an adequate interpretation of life, and that morality alone can make it worthy of respect and admiration. This is the characteristic American way of looking at the complicated and interesting business of living which we men and women have upon our hands.

It is rather a sober and intense view. It is not always free from prejudice, from bigotry, from fanaticism, from superstition. It is open to invasion by strange and uncouth forms of religiosity. America has offered a fertile soil for the culture of new and queer religions. But on the whole,—yes, in immensely the larger proportion,—the old religion prevails, and a rather simple and primitive type of Christianity keeps its hold upon the hearts and minds of the majority. The consequence of this is (to quote again from Professor Münsterberg, lest you should think me a prejudiced reporter), that "however many sins there are, the life of the people is intrinsically pure, moral, and devout." "The number of those who live above the general level of moral requirement is astonishingly large."

Now this habit of soul, this tone of life, is reflected in American literature. Whatever defects it may have, a lack of serious feeling and purpose is not among them. It is pervaded, generally, by the spiritual preconception. It approaches life from the point of view of responsibility.

It gives full value to those instincts, desires, and hopes in man which have to do with the unseen world.

Even in those writers who are moved by a sense of revolt against the darkness and severity of certain theological creeds, the attempt is not to escape from religion, but to find a clearer, nobler, and more loving expression of religion. Even in those works which deal with subjects which are non-religious in their specific quality,—stories of adventure, like Cooper's novels; poems of romance, like the ballads of Longfellow and Whittier,—one feels the implication of a spiritual background, a moral law, a Divine providence,—

> "Standeth God within the shadow, keeping
> watch above his own."

This, hitherto, has been the characteristic note of the literature of America. It has taken for granted that there is a God, that men must answer to Him for their actions, and that one of the most interesting things about people, even in books, is their moral quality.

(2) Another trait which seems to me strongly marked in the American temperament and clearly reflected in American literature is the love of nature. The attractions of the big out-of-doors have taken hold upon the people. They feel a strong affection for their great, free, untended forests, their swift-rushing rivers, their bright, friendly brooks, their wooded mountain ranges of the East, their snowy peaks and vast plains and many-coloured canyons of the West.

I suppose there is no other country in the world where so many people break away from the fatigues of civilization every year, and go out to live in the open for a vacation with nature. The business of making tents and camp outfits for these voluntary gypsies has grown to be enormous. In California they do not even ask for a tent. They sleep *à la belle étoile*.

The Audubon societies have spread to every State. You will not find anywhere in Europe, except perhaps in Switzerland, such companies of boys and girls studying the wild flowers and the birds. The interest is not altogether, nor mainly, scientific. It is vital and temperamental. It is the expression of an inborn sympathy with nature and a real delight in her works.

This has found an utterance in the large and growing "nature-literature" of America. John James Audubon, Henry Thoreau, John Burroughs, Clarence King, John Muir, Ernest Seton, Frank Chapman, Ernest Ingersoll,—these are some of the men who have not only carefully described, but also lovingly interpreted, "nature in her visible forms," and so have given to their books, beyond the value of accurate records of observation, the charm of sympathetic and illuminative writing.

But it is not only in these special books that I would look for evidence of the love of nature in the American temperament. It is found all through the poetry and the prose of the best writers. The most perfect bit of writing in the works of that stern Calvinist, Jonathan Edwards, is the description of an early morning walk through a field of wild flowers. Some of the best pages of Irving and Cooper are sketches of landscape along the Hudson River. The scenery of New England is drawn with infinite delicacy and skill in the poetry of Bryant, Whittier, and Emerson. Bret Harte and Joaquin Miller make as see the painted desert and the ragged Sierras. James Lane Allen shows us the hemp fields of Kentucky, George Cable the bayous of Louisiana. But the list of illustrations is endless. The whole literature of America is filled with pictures of nature. There is hardly a familiar bird or flower for which some poet has not tried to find a distinct, personal, significant expression in his verse.

(3) A third trait of the American temperament is the sense of humour. This is famous, not to say notorious. The Americans are supposed to be a nation of jokers, whose daily jests, like their ready-made shoes, have a peculiar oblique form which makes it slightly difficult for people of other nationalities to get into them.

There may be some truth in the latter part of this supposition, for I have frequently observed that a remark which seemed to me very amusing only puzzled a foreigner. For example, a few years ago, when Mark Twain was in Europe, a despatch appeared in some of the American newspapers giving an account of his sudden death. Knowing that this would trouble his friends, and being quite well, he sent a cablegram in these words, "Report of my death grossly exaggerated, Mark Twain." When I repeated this to an Englishman, he looked at me pityingly and said: "But how could you exaggerate a thing like that, my dear fellow? Either he was dead, or he was alive, don't you know." This was perfectly incontestable, and the statement of it represented the English point of view.

But to the American incontestable things often have a double aspect: first that of the solemn fact; and then that of the curious, unreal, pretentious shape in which it is dressed by fashion, or vanity, or stupid respectability. In this region of incongruities created by the contrast between things as they really are and the way in which dull or self-important people usually talk about them, American humour plays.

It is not irreverent toward the realities. But for the conventionalities, the absurdities, the pomposities of life, it has a habit of friendly satire and good-tempered raillery. It is not like the French wit, brilliant and pointed. It is not like the English fun, in which practical joking plays so large a part. It is not like the German joke, which announces its arrival with the sound of a trumpet. It usually wears rather a sober face and speaks with a quiet voice. It delights in exposing pretensions by gravely carrying them to the point of wild extravagance. It finds its material in subjects which are laughable, but not odious; and in people who are ridiculous, but not hateful.

Its favourite method is to exaggerate the foibles of persons who are excessive in certain directions, or to make a statement absurd simply by taking it literally. Thus a Yankee humorist said of a certain old lady that she was so inquisitive that she put her head out of all the front windows of the house at the same time. A Westerner claimed the prize of inventiveness for his town on the ground that one of its citizens had taught his ducks to swim on hot water in order that they might lay boiled eggs. Mr. Dooley described the book in which President Roosevelt gave his personal reminiscences of the Spanish-American War under the title *"Alone in Cubea."*

Once, when I was hunting in the Bad Lands of North Dakota, and had lost my way, I met a solitary horseman in the desert and said to him, "I want to go to the Cannonball River." "Well, stranger," he answered, looking at me with a solemn air of friendly interest, "I guess ye can go if ye want to; there ain't no string on ye." But when I laughed and said what I really wanted was that he should show me the way, he replied, "Why didn't ye say so?" and rode with me until we struck the trail to camp.

All this is typical of native American humour, quaint, good-natured, sober-faced, and extravagant. At bottom it is based upon the democratic assumption that the artificial distinctions and conventional phrases of life are in themselves amusing. It flavours the talk of the street and the dinner-table. It makes the Americans inclined to prefer farce to melodrama, comedietta to grand opera. In its extreme and degenerate form it drifts into habitual buffoonery, like the crude, continuous jests of the comic supplements to the Sunday newspapers. In its better shape it relieves the strenuousness and the monotony of life by a free and kindly touch upon its incongruities, just as a traveller on a serious errand makes the time pass by laughing at his own mishaps and at the queer people whom he meets by the way.

You will find it in literature in all forms: in books of the professional humorists from Artemus Ward to Mr. Dooley: in books of *genre* painting, like Mark Twain's *Huckleberry Finn* and *Pudd'nhead Wilson*, or like *David Harum*, which owed its immense popularity to the lifelike portrait of an old horse trader in a rural town of central New York: in books of sober purpose, like the essays of Lowell or Emerson, where a sudden smile flashes out at you from the gravest page. Oliver Wendell Holmes shows it to you, in *The Autocrat of the Breakfast Table*, dressed in the proper garb of Boston; you may recognize it on horseback among the cowboys, in the stories of Owen Wister and O. Henry; it talks the Mississippi River dialect in the admirable pages of Charles D. Stewart's *Partners with Providence*, and speaks with the local accent of Louisville, Kentucky, in *Mrs. Wiggs of the Cabbage Patch*. Almost everywhere you will find the same general tone, a compound of mock gravity, exaggeration, good nature, and inward laughter.

You may catch the spirit of it all in a letter that Benjamin Franklin sent to a London newspaper in 1765. He was having a little fun with English editors who had been printing wild articles about America. "All this," wrote he, "is as certainly true as the account, said to be from Quebec, in all the papers of last week, that the inhabitants of Canada are making preparations for a cod and whale fishery this summer in the upper Lakes. Ignorant people may object that the upper Lakes are fresh, and that cod and whales are salt-water fish; but let them know, Sir, that cod, like other fish, when attacked by their enemies, fly into any water where they can be safest; that whales, when they have a mind to eat cod, pursue them wherever they fly; and that the grand leap of the whale in the chase up the Falls of Niagara is esteemed, by those who have seen it, as one of the finest spectacles in Nature."

(4) The last trait of the American temperament on which I wish touch briefly is the sentiment of humanity.

It is not an unkind country, this big republic, where the manners are so "free and easy," the *tempo* of life so quick, the pressure of business so heavy and continuous. The feeling of philanthropy in its broader sense,—the impulse which makes men inclined to help one another, to sympathize with the unfortunate, to lift a neighbour or a stranger out of a tight place,—good will, in short,—is in the blood of the people.

When their blood is heated, they are hard hitters, fierce fighters. But give them time to cool down, and they are generous peacemakers. Abraham Lincoln's phrase, "With malice toward none, with charity for all," strikes the key-note. In the "mild concerns of ordinary life" they like to cultivate friendly relations, to show neighbourliness, to do the useful thing.

There is a curious word of approbation in the rural dialect of Pennsylvania. When the country folk wish to express their liking for a man, they say, "He is a very common person,"—meaning not that he is low or vulgar, but approachable, sympathetic, kind to all.

Underneath the surface of American life, often rough and careless, there lies this widespread feeling: that human nature everywhere is made of the same stuff; that life's joys and sorrows are felt in the same way whether they are hidden under homespun and calico or under silk and broadcloth; that it is every man's duty to do good and not evil to those who live in the world with him.

In literature this feeling has shown itself in many ways. It has given a general tone of sympathy with "the under dog in a fight." It has led writers to look for subjects among the plain people. It has made the novel of American "high life" incline generally to satire or direct rebuke. In the typical American romance the hero is seldom rich, the villain seldom poor.

In the weaker writers the humane sentiment dwindles into sentimentality. In the stronger writers it gives, sometimes, a very noble and manly note. In general you may say that it has impressed upon American literature the mark of a moral purpose,—the wish to elevate, to purify, to fortify the mind, and so the life, of those who read.

Is this a merit or a fault in literature? Judge for yourselves.

No doubt a supremely ethical intention is an insufficient outfit for an author. His work may be

> "Chaste as the icicle
> That's curded by the frost from purest snow
> And hangs on Dian's temple,"

and yet it may be without savour or permanence. Often the desire to teach a good lesson bends a book from the straight line of truth-to-the-facts, and makes a so-called virtuous ending at the price of sincerity and thoroughgoing honesty.

It is not profitable to real virtue to dwell in a world of fiction where miracles are worked to crown the good and proper folk with unvarying felicity and to send all the rascals to prison or a miserable grave. Nor is it a wise and useful thing for literature to ignore the lower side of life for the sake of commending the higher; to speak a false and timid language for fear of shocking the sensitive; to evade the actual problems and conflicts which men and women of flesh and blood have to meet, for the sake of creating a perfectly respectable atmosphere for the imagination to live in.

This mistaking of prudery for decency, this unwillingness to deal quite frankly with life as it is, has perhaps acted with a narrowing and weakening effect upon the course of American literature in the past. But just now there seems to be a reaction toward the other extreme. Among certain English and American writers, especially of the female sex, there is a new fashion of indiscriminate candour which would make Balzac blush. But I suppose that this will pass, since every extreme carries within itself the seed of disintegration.

The *morale* of literature, after all, does not lie outside of the great circle of ethics. It is a simple application of the laws which embrace the whole of human life to the specific business of a writer.

To speak the truth; to respect himself and his readers; to do justly and to love mercy; to deal with language as a living thing of secret and incalculable power; not to call good, evil, or evil, good; to honour the noble and to condemn the base; to face the facts of life with courage, the humours of life with sympathy, and the mysteries of life with reverence; and to perform his task of writing as carefully, as lovingly, as well as he can,—this, it seems to me, is the whole duty of an author.

This, if I mistake not, has been the effort of the chief writers of America. They have spoken surely to the heart of a great people. They have kept the fine ideals of the past alive in the conflicts of the present. They have lightened the labours of a weary day. They have left their readers a little happier, perhaps a little wiser, certainly a little stronger and braver, for the battle and the work of life.

The measure of their contribution to the small group of world-books, the literature that is universal in meaning and enduring in form, must be left for the future to determine. But it is sure already that American literature has done much to express and to perpetuate the Spirit of America.

[1] The lectures which followed, at the Sorbonne, on Irving, Cooper, Bryant, Poe, Longfellow, Hawthorne, Whittier, Emerson, Lowell, Whitman, and Present Tendencies in American Literature, are not included in this volume.

HERBERT CROLY'S

The Promise of American Life

Cloth, 12mo, $2.00 net

PRESIDENT J. G. SCHURMAN OF CORNELL UNIVERSITY writes of this book: "I regard Mr. Croly's book as a serious and weighty contribution to contemporary American politics. A treatise on the fundamental political ideas of the American people which attempts to develop their full content and to re-read American history in the light of these developed ideas cannot, of course, be made light literature; but the author brings to the weighty subject with which he deals a lucid and vivacious style and a logical sense of arrangement. And thoughtful readers who are interested in fundamental political principles, once they have started the book, are pretty certain to finish it.... For my own part I have found the book exceedingly stimulating. It is also instructive, for the author seems to be thoroughly versed in the modern political and economic history not only of America but of Europe as well. Finally, the volume has the immense attraction of dealing with a subject which of all political subjects is now most prominent in the mind not only of thoughtful citizens, but, one might almost say, of the American people."

"'The Promise of American Life' will beyond doubt be recognized by students of the great philosophical currents of American history and political development as an unusual and remarkable work.... Mr. Croly acutely analyzes American democracy and pseudo-democracy, while his treatment of the actual present tendencies of democratic ideals is even more instructive and suggestive than the purely historical part of his book. He writes with a free pen and is both apt and keen-witted in his way of illustrating theories and beliefs by practical applications. One chapter, for instance, which will attract very special attention is that which considers the aims and methods of four typical reformers, Jerome, Hearst, Bryan, and Roosevelt."—*The Outlook.*

Milton Keynes UK
Ingram Content Group UK Ltd.
UKHW050650260624
444769UK00004B/205